CW00540079

Arc

Alejandro de la Sota

The Architecture of Imperfection

John Deeke March 3rd 2002

Alejandro de la Sota 1913–1996
The Architecture of Imperfection
Authors: Alejandro de la Sota,
Iñaki Abalos, Javier Castañón,
William Curtis, José Manuel
López-Peláez, Mohsen Mostafavi

This publication has been
produced to accompany an
exhibition held at the
Architectural Association in
London from 4–21 June 1997.
Both publication and exhibition
have been initiated by the
Chairman, Mohsen Mostafavi,
with the assistance of
Javier Castañón.

The publication has been edited
by Pamela Johnston and
designed by Nicola Bailey and
Dennis Bailey. It has been
produced through the AA Print
Studio with Marilyn Sparrow
(art assistant), Charlotte Coudrille
and Suzanna Prizeman (editorial
assistants).

ISBN 1 870890 74 4

Printed in England
by Spin Offset Ltd.

Contents © 1997
Architectural Association
and the Authors
AA Publications
34–36 Bedford Square
London WC1B 3ES

No part of this book may be used
or reproduced in any manner
without written permission from
the publisher, except in the
context of reviews.

Alejandro de la Sota is part of the
AA Exemplary Projects series.
Other titles in the series include
*Thermal Bath at Vals by
Peter Zumthor,* and *Free
University, Berlin.*

COVER AND INSIDE FRONT COVER
Details of Bankunión headquarters model.
Photos: Fundación Alejandro de la Sota

Acknowledgements

The Architectural Association would like to express its gratitude to the Fundación Alejandro de la Sota, and in particular to José de la Sota, for its whole-hearted support of the publication and the related exhibition. We would also like to thank Juan de la Sota and Alejandro de la Sota for assisting in the design of the exhibition.

Photographs
The majority of photographs in this publication were specially commissioned from Etienne Clément. Archival photographs are reproduced with the permission of the Fundación Alejandro de la Sota.

Photo credits
Etienne Clement: 19, 25, 26, 27, 30 (above), 32, 46, 47, 48, 52, 67, 87, 88, 89, 90, 91, 92–3, 94, 95, 100, 109, 110, 111
Fundación Alejandro de la Sota: 8, 20, 30 (below), 33, 35, 38, 39, 44, 68, 69, 77, 79, 81, 83, 86, 97, 101, 108, 109
José Manuel López-Peláez: 34, 37, 40, 43
José de la Sota: 38

Translations
Translations are by Javier Castañón (The problem of Architecture), Emma Holmes (Alejandro de la Sota: the construction of an architect), Mark Vernon-Jones (Viewing Sota).

Exhibition
The AA would like to acknowledge the financial contribution made by the Banco Central Hispano, London, towards the exhibition.
AA exhibitions organizer: Linda Brown
Gallery manager: Andrew Mackenzie

Demythologizing the real

Mohsen Mostafavi

Alejandro de la Sota is one of Spain's foremost architects of the recent past. He is part of a generation whose work exhibits a direct continuity with early modernism and the project of modernity. These architects, most of whom began their careers soon after the Second World War, lacked the dogmatism of the early avant-garde but nevertheless pursued many of its concerns and had in turn to confront its critical repercussions. The impact of industrialization and hence the issue of repetition; individuality vs. impersonality; monumentality; and a more general questioning of the role of technology – the topics of debate during this period remain justifiably relevant to contemporary practice.

The work of Alejandro de la Sota directly explores these concerns. While clearly acknowledging the significant contribution of the 'masters' – Wright, Le Corbusier, Mies – his approach is deliberately less singular and polemical (not that his work cannot be polemicized). Throughout his life de la Sota designed and constructed projects that at first glance appear more empirical and pragmatic than ideological.

One can detect a similarity of intent between the work of de la Sota and that of Team X, to which his friend and contemporary José Antonio Coderch belonged. For that group, the war resulted in the necessity for an architecture of austerity, which would achieve the best possible solution with limited material and technical resources. De la Sota's commitment to what he termed architectural 'simplicity' is wholly in keeping with this aim, but, as with the most interesting of the Team X projects, his solutions are invariably dependent on the transgression of those very limits, whether material or technical.

De la Sota's own version of this condition is best exemplified by his recollection of a chance encounter with Le Corbusier in the 1950s, during the construction of the unité d'habitation in Berlin. He was struck by Le Corbusier's renunciation of the German builders' constant drive towards perfection: 'It looked as if they [the builders] had passed their tongues over the concrete before letting it set', he recalls Corb saying.

For Alejandro de la Sota, who was used to the less than perfect standards of construction in Spain after the war, Le Corbusier's call for an architecture of 'imperfection' provided a crucial inspiration. It was this apparent quest for imperfection which gave his work its 'elegance'. Equally, imperfection resisted the ideality of the image as the a-priori task of architecture.

In the Arvesù house on the calle Doctor Arce in Madrid of 1955, de la Sota developed an inward-looking architecture which, partly in response to the conditions of the site, 'turned its back on the world'. He claimed that if it had been left to him he would not have placed a single window on the street facade: a compromise with the client resulted in a few small openings. Regardless, the rough undulating brick walls of the facade assume a mass reminiscent of baroque architecture; the silence of these walls is heightened by the modulations of sunlight on their uneven surfaces. The building demonstrates the value of reticence: hence de la Sota's mistrust of 'representation' as the prioritization of the visual, his denial of the necessity for architecture to act as the conveyor of messages.

While completing the Arvesù house, de la Sota was also involved in the construction of the Gobierno Civil (Civil Government) building in Tarragona, which he had won in competition. This public project would not allow him to avoid representation. Instead it provided him with the opportunity to confront one of the main dilemmas of modern architecture during this period: namely, the question of monumentality. The need for a new monumentality, as articulated by Sigfried Giedion among others, concerns modern architecture's response to the role of public or symbolic buildings, as distinct from the appearance of the architecture of housing, supposedly derived purely from the consideration of rational necessities.

The Gobierno Civil in Tarragona had to represent the central government in that province. Finding a means to combine civic and residential uses was the challenge of the project. In de la Sota's initial sketches the different functions are separated into a horizontal and a vertical block, with a garden in between. The final design combines these uses in a single block, while adding a secondary group of residences on the ground floor. Though the side elevations have many windows, de la Sota, in a similar manner to the Arvesù house, keeps the main elevation primarily opaque, working with the symmetry and asymmetry of deep recesses to create an overall tension and balance. This gives the impression of a crack, a fault line in the mass of the marble which in turn reveals the dark surfaces of glass and metal set back from the outer limit of the building.

The 'imperfection' of the main elevation is achieved through the shifting of the two middle openings to the left and right of the facade's central axis. However, the openings still share an edge, a line in the depth of the building which appears as a single point on the facade – a 'weak' joint denying the structural logic of the facade's visuality and at the same time creating its point of balance. De la Sota's bringing together of the various configurations rests on his denial of rationality as a form of reductivism. According to the philosopher Ernesto Grassi:

There is a radical difference in the attitude toward reality between those who are logically persuaded to attain reality by defining it in logical terms – that is, by means of rational metaphysics of onto-theology – and those who, like Joyce, start from a statement of the real as it ingeniously 'unveils' itself, a reality that is not to be rationally 'explained', but only 'described'.[1]

The reality that is born from de la Sota's ingenious juxtaposition of the different materials – marble, glass, metal – sets up associations that are not unconscious but involve a new unveiling of the real, from which metonymic descriptions stem. This form of reality cannot be explained, but only described; in the words of Grassi, 'the real is recognized as inexplicable'.

The Maravillas Gymnasium – probably the most significant demonstration of de la Sota's ideas – is an architecture born out of the resolution and adjustment of all the necessities of the project, including an awkward site and limited financial and material resources. As de la Sota has said, 'there was little time to worry about a specific Architecture, which is why the building does not have any Architecture at all ... or perhaps that is an Architecture in itself.'

One can assume that the construction of this project relies on de la Sota's notions of a 'logical architecture', by which he means studying all the far-ranging implications of a project before developing possible ways of resolving the puzzle of the building. In this task the relation between materials and solutions is of importance. The design is informed by the choice of particular materials as well as the specific ways in which they are used. Equally, the particularities of each project afford new opportunities in the choice and manner of use of materials. This is one of the distinguishing characteristics of the work of de la Sota – each project is begun anew, without any stylistic preoccupations or continuities. His archi-

1. Ernesto Grassi, 'Joyce and Vico: The Demythologization of the Real', in *Vico and Joyce*, ed. by Donald Phillip Verene, Albany, N.Y., 1987, p. 157.

tecture is predicated on constructing interruptions – discontinuities.

De la Sota's constant reference to materials is part of his more general belief in the need for new techniques. It is the inventive use of these techniques, as well as the transformation of existing technologies, which produces the architectures of his projects. De la Sota's method bears some resemblance to art practices of the early part of the twentieth century, particularly those of certain constructivist artists. His method of working is more akin to Tatlin's assemblages, for example, than it is to Picasso's collages. The former rely on the possibilities of materials and their juxtaposition to invent the form of the objects, while the latter recall images of existing objects of everyday use – a chair, guitar, etc. – in order for these to be seen differently. However, de la Sota's constructions, like those of Tatlin, do not begin with but rather move towards the visual – the project's appearance, its form, is arrived at through the particularity of its virtual and physical construction.

In the Maravillas Gymnasium the visuality is formed by the extension of the existing upper courtyard on to the roof, the sectional solution allowing both light and air into the sports hall and the classrooms. The architecture and the structure are bound together, constructing and structuring each other. The structuring of the project relies on its fabrication, as much as its fabrication relies on its programmatic, sociological, economic, material and technological circumstances.

Since the circumstances of each project are different, de la Sota feels obliged to invent new solutions. What remains constant in all his projects is the commitment to using new techniques as enabling frameworks for architecture. He does not adopt technology in a totalizing or dominating manner, but rather utilizes specific techniques to modify and subsequently invent new forms of spatial relations. It is the uniqueness and the particularity of each solution which resist, interrupt, the subjugating logic of abstract technology.

The design for the residential college in Orense of 1967 exemplifies this approach. De la Sota proposed the use of 'repeated multi-use volumetric modules' made of pre-stressed concrete with different interior finishes. The smaller components – windows, doors, etc. – were based on details from the railway and coachwork industry. It is the adaptions of the repetitive units to the sloping terrain – the suspension of a single abstract datum – as well as the influence of other vernacular constructions from de la Sota's homeland of Galicia, which transform the constructive logic of the modules.

Thus de la Sota avoids the pitfalls of much contemporary practice by designing buildings which, despite their uniqueness, still carry something of the everyday – of the anonymous world of industrial products, of other houses, gymnasia and offices. In a world so eager for representation, the architecture of Alejandro de la Sota seems justly poised between reticence and invention – a new unveiling of the real.

The problem of Architecture

Alejandro de la Sota

A previously unpublished description by Alejandro de la Sota of his approach to teaching and philosophy of Architecture, with an introduction and commentaries by Javier Castañón.

In Spain the figure of Alejandro de la Sota is that of a master: a master builder, but also a master teacher. His impact on the Madrid School of Architecture, where he taught from 1956 to 1972, is even today hard to quantify. His lectures filled the school's main auditorium, as students from every department, not just those officially enrolled in his course, would make sure they found time to attend. I was then studying at Madrid, and saw how his teaching became the focus of conversation among students. Naturally, I also visited his buildings and was impressed to discover how he had translated into built form the elements of his lectures, the lessons illustrated with reference to the architecture of the 'masters', and typically never his own.

Through his work and his teaching de la Sota profoundly influenced the course of architecture in Spain. International recognition came in the late 1970s and early 1980s, when critics began to describe him as one of the three masters of Spanish architecture this century, linking his name with those of Coderch and Sáenz de Oíza. In this light an investigation of de la Sota's life, work and pedagogic method becomes all the more pressing.

I have had the good fortune to receive from Alejandro de la Sota's studio the text that he submitted to the selection panel when he applied for the chair at the Madrid School of Architecture in 1971. Having translated this text, which is like a manifesto, I have added some notes to put it into perspective. It is my duty to honour one to whom I owe a debt of learning.

I first approached Don Alejandro in the academic year 1969/70, to ask permission to attend his lecture course even though I was not officially his student. The request was merely a pretext to enable me to establish a direct relationship with him. The ploy worked, and that year I not only attended his lecture course and design studio, but was in and out of his office at will. I remember quite well a number of conversations I had with him then: the occasion when he told me off for working up the early sketches of a project to make them appear more attractive, our discussion of a choice of school in Britain months before my departure, and so on. When I read his text now

I can see that his proposed teaching programme was a statement of principles that he had managed to translate into built form. For me, this great consonance between de la Sota's teaching and his work is the secret of his mastery.

The first explanatory note relates to the origin of the text. In the early 1970s the procedure governing the appointment of university professors was like something out of the nineteenth century. Each candidate, in competition, had to sit a kind of examination. The first statutory submission was an essay putting forward a teaching programme, a discourse on methodology, and a taught syllabus. In general such essays were formal addresses. De la Sota's text is, on the contrary, a straightforward description of his teaching during the previous decade, followed by a summary of his attitude towards his pupils. It is expressed in a language which is in places minimal, like the detailing of his buildings, but very often so dense that its full meaning is obtainable only upon a second or third reading – just like the 'programmes' of his buildings. Whenever de la Sota was asked to define architecture, he would simply smile, shrug his shoulders, and turn his body as if to embrace the whole surrounding world, saying something like: 'Everything around us is Architecture. Can you not perceive it in your mind? You may need to learn how to discover it, but it is already there. Now, if you are asking me how to be true to Architecture... that's something I can answer!'. And so he begins his text:

Forming a definition is a strange and complicated task, yet it makes no sense to tackle the problem of teaching methods without first defining what has already been taught.

A dogmatic definition of Architecture has no validity today. Any definition is formed by means of words – words that, in turn, have to be defined in terms of other words, and so on... Clearly this process leads us to undefined terms that none the less need to be understood.

As in the exact sciences, the most certain definition is an operative one: a definition that arises from a full consideration of the problems specific to architecture and architectural education.

It is possible to practise our profession and make no greater effort than that of seeing the job through construction. But a full commitment to Architecture implicitly requires us to be aware of, and to respond to, the things that are happening in the world today. This prompts a feeling of unease, as we contemplate an uncertain future. Everything is evolving rapidly; every event is already history. We are experiencing advance – analogical, total advance.

In some cases this advance is self-defining, as in aviation, for example. The aeroplane is held up by its 'advance', its movement through the air; this is basic. Further characteristics such as manoeuvrability, velocity and maximum ceiling are products of new techniques, always based upon the principle of movement.

And yet we see Architecture stuck, stranded, anchored in a past, a culture, with no projection towards any future.

Le Corbusier:[1] 'Only in Architecture is progress not indispensable; laziness reigns, everything is referred to the past. In everything else the uncertainty of the future propels us towards a

1. I have retained De la Sota's own translations rather than use the precise words of the original quotations because very often a more liberal interpretation was intended. De la Sota could read French and German and in his lectures he often quoted Le Corbusier, Mies, Gropius and Breuer from memory.

solution: without progress, we move closer to bankruptcy. But in Architecture there is no such thing as bankruptcy! A privileged profession! So there!'

We should take heed of the analogy of the aeroplane, for one of the main tasks facing architects today is that of turning their own advance, their own movement, their own intellectual development into something so intrinsic that it cannot be undone.

New needs inevitably arise, as do new means of fulfilling them; but the results we achieve are never totally satisfactory. Who could doubt that there is a logic to everything? Society, humanity as a whole, has its own logic; but it opposes our applied intelligence, basing its judgement on one important, simple fact – that of having been born with Architecture.

Architecture has become marginalized because it is not fully integrated into today's technological world, on account of its origin, its historical baggage, its character of permanence. New developments are due, almost entirely, to cultural movements.

Like the rest of science and technology, Architecture must now reflect on its own essence, look for its own means of development, create its own techniques. It can no longer live in the past; all the contributions made by other fields – by philosophy, technology, psychology and sociology – must become part of Architecture, and give it new form.[2]

A feeling for these professional, social and educational concerns draws one towards the school as the place where they may be shared, and indeed must be inculcated. To feel a vocation for teaching is to respond to one of the greatest doubts; it becomes difficult to conceive of another vocation.[3] Albers never was able to find an answer to the question: 'What is the difference between teaching and learning?' Le Corbusier expressed the same doubt when he said: 'Anything that can be taught is not worth learning.'

By remaining in education, one commits oneself to a state of constant unease which can be mitigated only by continuing to teach.

Learning is a process of internalization: the explication of a concept prompts ideas which are absorbed by the student and converted into personal thoughts.[4] The components of this process are a) the teacher, b) objective methods of explication, c) the student. We can no longer have recourse to the Academic method of teaching, which consists in imparting to the student a theory of Architecture with a defined set of principles and norms. These norms no longer exist, we have to create them anew.

Teaching (learning) is a risky undertaking for both teacher and student; it entails a day-to-day sharing of doubts – a joint work of two minds, one of them more experienced.[5]

The practice of Architecture requires us to deal with highly differentiated ideas and forms. Consequently, we are under an obligation to be consistent, coherent. It is important for the student to discover integrity and honesty; it is important, indeed obligatory, for the master to make the effort to match works with ideas. Difficult. A whole empty language has been born; we must look for new solutions, as yet without a name.

One of the difficulties of teaching is to strike the right balance between thought, building, and explanation. Frequently nowadays there is an imbalance towards, for example, explanation –

2. 'New technology' was a term that de la Sota often joked about: technology was a means to an end, he insisted, and therefore it was always new. When he submitted his proposal for the Bankunión headquarters (a building clad totally in glass with no external mullions or transoms), the client asked if anything like it had been done before. He answered that, to his knowledge, nothing like it had yet been built, though the idea itself was hardly new – and he referred to Mies van der Rohe. In the end the client decided not to go ahead with what would have been a great building: neither client nor architect knew that construction would begin barely fourteen months later on the smooth glass facades of Foster's Willis Faber Dumas headquarters in Ipswich.

However, it is the Maravillas Gymnasium that provides the most remarkable example of de la Sota's approach. At the time of its construction Spain was still recovering from the Civil War, isolated from foreign industrial power and technology. Rolled steel was extremely scarce, and came only in the form of flat sections of a standard size and thickness. The huge trusses were therefore produced by welding one flat section to another (mostly on site). The construction was a demonstration of true craftsmanship, ingenuity and inventiveness.

For de la Sota, the important thing was to know what had to be done: technology was only the means to achieve it.

3. De la Sota's social concerns were intimately tied to his profound understanding of human nature. He had lived through a cruel fratricidal war that had left Spain devastated, and in the early years of his career learned the importance of the architect's role in the re-building of entire towns and villages. Projects such as Esquivel Village show how he saw sociology and related disciplines as an integral part of the architect's cultural formation.

4. 'Internalization' in this sense is, I suspect, a word of de la Sota's own coining. He scorned the idea of learning by rote; memory was a resource to be enjoyed, not a tool for improving examination results.

5. 'One of them more experienced': de la Sota often expressed himself with disarming humility. The more categorical the students were about their little 'discoveries', the more respectful he would become with his suggestions. In this way he always achieved the desired effect: they would go home and mull over his words and reach the conclusions that he expected them to reach.

an emphasis on rhetoric rather than the authentic truth to be found in the pairing of thought with building. This is to confuse the means with the end.[6]

Teaching presupposes a transmission of principles from teacher to student: this transference will occur naturally if the teacher demonstrates the congruence of thought and building. But the value of the built example has to be clearly understood.

The transference from teacher to pupil depends upon a new tool: systematization.

A process of systematic internalization is used effectively in teaching science, which is simultaneously hypothetical, analytical and experimental. We may also apply this method to Architecture, provided that we introduce an intermediary element: systematic design. This is because the experimental aspect of the method can be proved only through Architecture itself, that is, through the built form: something that is to be made. In this way we bring to Architecture a constant element of risk.[7]

Our students are far from well prepared, psychologically, to embark upon Architecture. One cannot help but wonder if students come to other professions with as many preconceived ideas as they do. A student of Physics or Astronomy arrives at university with an open mind about their discipline. Our students bring with them a great, deeply engrained distortion, which in some cases they never manage to lose.

From birth, and even before it, man is immersed in Architecture both good and bad. He is marked psychologically, conditioned by it, right from the womb – the first Architecture that he comes to know.

Yet Architecture has lost its way in this world; a title is scarcely all that is needed to practise.

There is talk of an alternative approach: it has been suggested that an introductory course be provided for potential Architecture students at some earlier stage, perhaps in the secondary school syllabus.

No. We want students who know nothing about Architecture to begin with, because this will enable them to make better work later on. We consider it a mistake to initiate them so early into the profession, even at an elementary level, without first having related it to the whole world in which we live. We prefer an intense intellectual preparation emphasizing comprehension of the general problems, with a slight bias or inclination towards our future work with them in Architecture, which subtly directs them towards our field. Buckminster Fuller is clear on this point: 'The issue is not to imagine a better society, but rather to strive for a better Architecture in order to achieve a more desirable society.' We all know what Fuller understands by 'Architecture', and we also know what he means by a better society; there is no equivocation.

Students come today ready to open themselves up to great change, for better or for worse. Such commitment has great potential. But it will yield little, indeed nothing, if it is not properly channelled. We have to fulfil our role in contributing to this change; we must be fully committed to this undertaking. At the same time it is necessary to point out that collective movements are permeated by errors and lies.

6. De la Sota was no polemicist. He declared his position on things in careful terms. Almost invariably this position was quite simple: the answer was to be found in nature, in the nature of things. His condemnation of the 'distractions' that we were exposed to as students was equally pointed and precise.

7. System, systematic, 'systematization': de la Sota's approach to teaching was rather like his approach to technology; systems were a means to an end.
  In this text de la Sota uses the Spanish 'didacta' in preference to the usual word for teacher. His method was not Socratic, but rather that of a mentor – a person who passed on to the student his love for Architecture. The fact that he was not by nature a passionate or impulsive man made his passion for Architecture (always written with a capital A) all the more acute. He expected results to be quantifiable, definite, accurate. Architecture was an art, but it had to be as exact as a science: for him, ambiguity was a synonym for the lack of understanding that resulted from a superficial approach.

All of this, it must be understood, takes place always within the world of Architecture, from which we never depart, from which we apprehend everything else.

If, for example, the personality of Gropius is made intelligible to students, it can greatly aid their professional development. Gropius is a very useful model, as he had an acute perception of the needs of his time, which he translated, in a clear manner, to the design of his buildings. If we add to this a meticulous, consistently straightforward analysis of the whole concept of the Bauhaus, we can provide an introduction to the significance of a coherent work; to the meaning of the one person within the context of the group, forgetting how little individuality means in our craft today. For it is only by taking part in society that we can be of use to it.[8]

It is difficult not to view one course as a part of the overall educational experience; this applies to the principles of our teaching, as well as to its end results. A comparison of our experience with that of other schools in Spain and abroad prompts a meditation on the theme of 'subjects'. Is the individual subject not but one part of a whole, corresponding to a specific period of time, in a process which is forever under way, forever continuing? Thus we begin to trigger in the minds of students a basic, retrospective way of viewing which allows them to make connections between disparate times and unrelated experiences and, in so doing, bring these into the present. A recapturing of the past, in the Proustian sense. This can be achieved by anyone, regardless of their 'age or condition'. Even those students lost in their childhood may be recovered – and then thrust into our complex world, our complete world.
In the first years we deal not with small ideas but with big ideas, expressed in basic, accessible terms. Saint Teresa used the simplest words to express the most difficult thing: her love for God. Mozart said: 'My music can be understood and enjoyed by the most uneducated person, yet it is also true that the most learned will encounter some difficulties with it.' This is the world in which we wish to operate.[9]

It is necessary to defer the joy that is experienced upon embarking on Architecture; to replace it with a quest to understand its problems, so that one day it can be fully enjoyed anew. Arising naturally during this period of learning are the 'Elements of Composition',[10] which are but the motifs, the parts that form the first 'whole' of the first year. Reiterated in more depth and with greater precision, they may equally form the basis of more advanced courses. The point is to arrive at a clear understanding of these elements, because they exist, because they are needed, because they are there to be known. Their function, as it has developed to date, is open to change; it may be improved, suppressed, or even replaced; all of these constantly changing elements, be they material, functional, or psychological, admit of analysis and synthesis.

It is precisely in this analysis and synthesis that systematization comes into its own. The teacher will suggest, from experience, possible means of realization. The analysis must take into account the anthropological hypotheses and the physiological, physical and psychological characteristics that define the subject of the analysis, whether it is a thing or a function. In this way the student will see each concept as having not only a symbolic meaning but also a clear sense of definition.

And in the synthesis, the first step must be to give clear shape to the process of systematization applicable to each particular case; the final result is largely dependent upon

8. I cannot recall an instance where de la Sota put forward his own work as an example, whereas the names of Le Corbusier, Mies and Gropius were constantly on his lips.

9. The text was written in an atmosphere of change. Like other European universities, Madrid was experiencing a period of student unrest. The Spanish Ministry of Education had proposed sweeping changes in many areas of the syllabus. A number of these were actually implemented, with the result that in any one year there would be some students following the 'Old Plan' (meaning the old syllabus), and some the new. De la Sota put forward his own radical alternative: '*talleres verticales*' (vertical workshops), in which students from different years would work together under the same master. However, in the context of the University of Madrid, which had a vast enrolment, low teacher/student ratios, and a rather Napoleonic overall structure, this idea was usually viewed as impracticable.
    When I decided to leave Madrid, I asked de la Sota's advice on studying in Britain. Despite Spain's relative isolation at that time, he knew about the efforts of architects and teachers elsewhere, and gave me a very clear view of the scene in London: he was aware of the AA and of Archigram.

10. 'Elements of Composition' was the title given to the 'projects' course under the New Plan.

this. To lose sight of the whole, on account of an excessive interest in the parts or even the process itself, would be a grave mistake. A warning is appropriate here: a great number of dubious ends have been pursued in the name of the process – the 'design process'!

It is evident that students must be in an absolutely pure state of mind before they undertake this work. They must therefore undergo a stage of preparation that will rid them of their prejudices. New students of Architecture are often manifestly restless, anxious to begin the business of 'design'. This is the way their minds work. Before beginning a task, however, it is necessary to know what has to be done: this seems elementary. And yet there is frequently an attempt to put graphic representations before knowledge, and then proceed to a critique of these representations – and live with the consequences. This seems wrong. We have to awaken respect for representation; it is something so serious that it can only be properly conveyed if it comes from within.

We have to inculcate a way of thinking directed towards the totality and its parts; a complete mental 'organicism'. It has to be seen that a project is the projection of that which exists, which exists clearly, in our mind. In the case of a conceptual project this alone would be sufficient, but if the idea is to be taken further, and given material form, a representation is required to make it comprehensible to others.

Need we spell out that nothing has to be invented or not invented; that everything has to be based on a continual acquisition of knowledge. Architecture – Invention? Imagination? Architecture and everything, or nothing. The single constant: knowledge. And once this is exhausted: accretion. This is one of the first stumbling blocks for the misdirected student: discipline, a recognition of the need for greater knowledge before the individual invention. Mies said 'Architecture is not a sand-pit for children and adults to play in.' We must inculcate an enormous respect, a knowledge of the rules of the game, as a means of acquiring the great discernment that results in true wisdom and, in some cases, great invention. If students come to understand the asceticism of Mies's 'less is more', they will gain a great deal from the course.[9]

We will speak about culture: the culture that was and the culture that will be – that eternally new frontier, the shock of the future. We will speak about the dangers of an unresponsive erudition: dead culture. About rationalization as a response to our existing culture and the one yet to come. About a means of methodically analysing all the things which have an impact on our lives and which require, again, an architectural response, at first simple, then complex, from within.

We will awaken – plant the first seeds of – a specialized vocation. We are frightened by the idea of excessive growth, of a huge number of architects, old and new, all practising our strange and diffuse profession (whether badly or well). We must bear a responsibility for the global saturation achieved by the mediocre and the charlatans, but may find comfort in the potential for good work by specialists with a natural understanding of the totality of architecture. Should these truths not be made evident from the start? A timely warning would restrain no one, but benefit many.

These fears and hopes are the first incentive for the student to define a method of study. But there is often a precocious love for the drawing board and neglect of theory that we find

9. I will never forget how once, in his office, he gave me a kindly but stern reprimand: 'Always remember that the only real line is the meeting of two planes; the rest ... out!'

repugnant. The best student is still seen to be the one who excels in design. There should be a greater knowledge of the individual's abilities across the range of subjects in the course.

The precocious love of drawing gives rise to something even more pernicious: the idea that the drawing board is a plaything. There is, as we have previously indicated, an excessive fondness for the graphic image; we believe this to be the root of countless problems. Even good, clear graphic representation becomes unacceptable when it is put above all else and undertaken purely for its own sake. The resultant damage is irreparable, and the student thus contaminated is usually incurable.

Nothing is aesthetic, in Architecture or anything else, if it is not an expression which comes from within: an internal impulse made manifest. All forms can be negated, every one of them, if they are not the result of such an approach. Our teaching has negated 'form'; we have difficulty even uttering the word in our lectures. But form is welcomed – namelessly – when it is a result. Everything has its form but it is never named as such except in the context of Art. And here we come to the crux of the problem, the big question. Architecture – a fine art? Do new fine arts exist? Or only those that existed before?

In the classroom we must put aside marginal problems and present those issues which may stimulate the growth of architectural thought. We must enrich the issues, saturate them, load them with data, view them from different angles – and then try to resolve them. Recurrent data – the product of experience, knowledge, investigation, shared communication – is fed into the 'black box' that is our brain. When the need arises, we can externalize this data, systematize it, using whatever means we have at our disposal, from the pencil to the computer, always proceeding, however, in a pragmatic manner, rationalizing in order to find new solutions; perhaps even a new 'fine art' within a new 'Architecture'.

'You do not bring about a revolution by the act of revolting, but by finding solutions', Le Corbusier.

Gobierno Civil — Proceso para su estudio en el caso concreto de Tarragona.

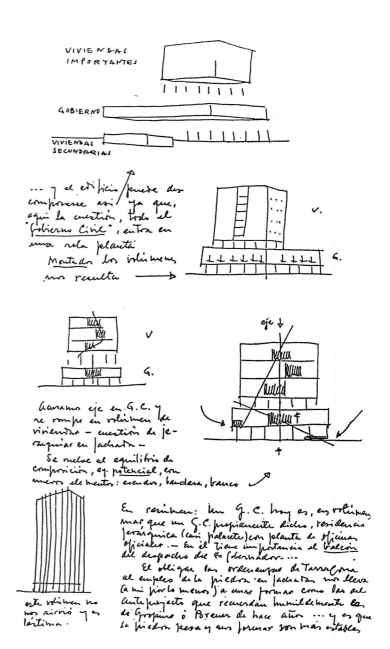

'Civil Government – Process of study in the concrete case of Tarragona'

'Harmonic, hierarchical and noble':
de la Sota's Civil Government building in Tarragona

William J. R. Curtis

Alejandro de la Sota belongs to the same generation as Jørn Utzon, Denys Lasdun, Aldo van Eyck and José Antonio Coderch, but it is only in recent years that his work has become known outside Spain. It is an oeuvre of impressive consistency, combining a naked abstraction with a rigorous interest in the character of materials. Hard facts of construction are rendered poetic through a control of form and a close attention to generating ideas. While de la Sota clearly drew many lessons from the modern masters – from Mies van der Rohe in particular – he also managed to define a language with an internal momentum of its own.[1]

It is an architecture in which the primary idea is central and in which the design process consists in paring away inessentials to reach some underlying image which lies close to the heart of the architect's programmatic interpretation. Each project is pervaded by a hierarchy of intentions which manifest themselves in the play of volumes and spaces, in the sequence of movements, in the choice of structural elements and materials, and in the handling of detail. The generator may lie in a particular feature such as the passage of light and air, as in the section of the Maravillas Gymnasium of 1960–62, or in the interpretation of an institution and a place, as seems to have been the case with the Civil Government building

(Gobierno Civil) of 1956–61. Thus there is a special interest in probing a single design by this architect: not only does this reveal the quality of architectural thought in a unique solution, but it also sheds light upon more general matters, such as de la Sota's evolving vocabulary, his debts to earlier modern architecture, and his capacity to translate social purpose into architectural form.

The Gobierno Civil is important for another reason: it provides an unusual case of a modern work of a high order working in the service of a conservative and dictatorial regime. The main symbolic function of the building was, in fact, to represent the central government of Madrid in the 'province' of Catalonia. The expression of state authority was intrinsic to the programme. Indeed, had de la Sota followed 'official' canons of the period, he might well have ended up with a hackneyed neo-classical solution, rather like the ministries in Madrid by Secundino Zuazo and others. But there was also an important intermediary approach represented by buildings such as the Madrid Ministry of Labour of 1949 by Francisco de Asís Cabrero and Rafael de Aburto. With its base, middle, and top, with its abstract grid of brickwork and its subdued classical allusions, this building suggests affiliations with the Italian rationalists of the 1930s and early 1940s.

Against this background, the Civil Govern-

1. For overviews of de la Sota's work see Miguel Angel Baldellou, *Alejandro de la Sota*, Madrid, 1975, in the series 'Artistas Espanoles Contemporaneos'. Also *Alejandro de la Sota*, Madrid, Pronaos, 1989.

ment building seems assertively 'modern' in its use of bold geometries, its hovering planes, its dynamic composition of solids and voids, its ambiguities and transparencies, its Miesian and Corbusian echoes. But, on closer inspection, the building is found to be suffused with classical analogies and subtle references to past conventions of civic monumentality. More than that, it is a work which hovers consciously upon the knife-edge between modernity and tradition, and in the process recasts the identity of both parties in the debate. What we seem to have here is a work rich in ambiguities which takes over the dead-weight of Francoist iconography and subverts it, in a teasing play of oppositions and polarities. Or, one could say that the Civil Government building casts the language of international modern architecture in a rhetorical mode in order to provide an idealized portrait of the role of the governor and of the relationship between state and people, building and city.[2]

Before analysing the building and the intentions behind it in detail, it is well to be aware of several intellectual obstacles which have stood in the way – quite understandably – of a balanced assessment of Spanish modernism of the Franco period. It should not be forgotten that some of the earliest accounts of modern architecture were written by historians who were themselves émigrés from dictatorial regimes or who were not likely, at any rate, to sympathize with anything produced under Fascism. There may even have been a tendency to regard liberal democracy as the only possible ground for an authentic modernism. By way of a corollary, it tended to be assumed that authoritarian states might only express themselves through a retrograde and oppressive traditionalism.

Whatever the political rights and wrongs of the situation, a certain historical distortion was liable to result. Figures such as the Italians Giuseppe Terragni and Adalberto Libera tended to be kept out of the account, only to be disinterred several decades later when suitably disinfected by formalist criticism of the neo-rationalist variety. With Spain, the matter was even more complicated because the country remained isolated from the 'liberal democratic' consensus of Western Europe and the United States in the post-war years. In the official legends of modernism it was

alright to talk about the 'good Spain' of Picasso's *Guernica*, or Sert's Spanish Pavilion of 1937, especially as these seemed to represent a worthy equation between political emancipation and modernism. But the Spain that stayed behind was out of bounds, and rested under a cloud of opprobrium in the 1950s, 1960s and 1970s. Only the odd Catalan, like Coderch, was able to slip away and join the international debate on architecture.

The Civil Government building touches upon these contradictions in several interesting ways, for it flies in the face of the stereotypes. Curiously, too, in terms of the mysterious power of certain works to transcend their original social and political situation, the building is now an object of great civic pride for the local Catalan government and the population of the city. Younger generations of architects, who might disapprove of the politics that it originally represented, now look upon it as an essential link back to the canonical works of international modernism.[3] In this scenario it emerges as a *tour de force* of poetic abstraction which demonstrates how modern Spanish architecture may sometimes take on a Mediterranean accent. Needless to say, this retrospective instatement runs its own risks of oversimplification, especially where the expression of state authority is concerned.

Before weaving any further interpretations around the building, it is well to look at the object itself. It stands on the north rim of a wide circular space known as the Imperial Tarraco. This is about a kilometre from the Mediterranean, not far from the entry point to the Lérida highway. Early photographs show that the building was then near the edge of the city, but its presence was clearly felt, even in a place studded with fine medieval and Roman monuments. Tourist maps of the 1960s include it with the usual historical landmarks. The site itself is wedge-shaped, with angled roads cutting past on both sides. The main facade faces almost due south, slightly off the axis of the Ramblas opposite, which runs straight down to the sea.

The first impression is of a statuesque block poised above deep-cut bands of shadow. The holes punched through the marble walls create a haunting, memorable figure. The building rises six storeys – seven, if one counts the small penthouse on top. The overall impression is vertical; however,

2. The interpretation of the Civil Government building offered here was presented in a lecture entitled 'Alejandro de la Sota and modernism in Spain' at E.T.H. Zurich in January 1990; since then the author has had a chance to scrutinize sketches and notes for the project in the Fundación Alejandro de la Sota archive in Madrid which have tended to confirm the interpretation originally made. For situation of the Civil Government building, and of de la Sota's *oeuvre* in the overall history of modern architecture, see William J. R. Curtis, *Modern Architecture Since 1900*, London, Phaidon, 1996, third edition, pp. 486–9.

3. See, for example, *Arquitectura Viva*, Madrid, November 1988, celebrating de la Sota's seventy-fifth birthday, especially the insightful article by Juan Navarro Baldeweg, 'Un Laborioso Abstracción', p. 29 ff.

Corner of facade at levels three and four

this is offset by the horizontal podium containing the main government functions, and by the low block to the rear containing a variety of public offices. The scale of the building is enough to dominate even a space as wide as the Imperial Tarraco, and its stance is enough to connect it to the city on the other side – even to address the sea from the land. This facade, with its taut marble sheets reflecting the sun, its gaping shaded openings, and its modern version of a Doge's 'benediction loggia', puts one in mind of a public palace projecting the state towards a wider Mediterranean world of influence.

The site of the building forms part of the edge of the circular Imperial Tarraco, but is also sliced off and separated from this space by the converging diagonal streets to either side. De la Sota's solution acknowledges this dual identity. Seen head-on, the Civil Government building presents a monumental urban screen of uncertain scale; it acts as a sort of planar backdrop to events in the plaza, though the facade is punctuated by protrusions and recessions. But seen from the diagonal, it reads very much as a freestanding urban block with front, back, and sides all treated differently. The side elevations, for example, are set flush with the stone veneers and are much less sculptural. The lower block of

offices to the rear expands into the wider part of the wedge-shaped site. But only in the slightest details does the building respond to the curvature of the plaza: the steel columns flanking the entrance are inflected to trace the geometry of the urban space. Through a certain intensity of form, through a degree of rhetoric in the figure of the main facade, the building dominates the entire space in front of it, even creating a tension between itself and the old city opposite.

The main external divisions of the building hint at the contents and the internal hierarchy. At the ground level is the entrance, tucked in under the main podium in a zone of shadow. This leads into a public assembly hall which gives broad views back on to the public square through its extensive glazing. The gesture recalls Terragni's Casa del Fascio in Como of 1932–6 as a way of bringing in public space under an institutional building. A lateral axis leads from this space towards a major stair that rises to the main government floor in the horizontal podium seen from outside, while the route straight ahead leads to the low block of offices to the rear with their more 'mundane' concerns. The main government floor is ample and dignified in scale. The governor's office is on the main axis behind the loggia seen in the facade. The same axis is once again accentuated at the fifth level, where the governor's master bedroom gives stunning views south across the town towards the sea.

The top of the podium provides a terrace which dominates the square and opens the institution to the surroundings for state occasions. It also registers the presence of quasi-public functions on the second floor (such as meeting rooms and conference hall) while inserting a strong caesura between the government areas of the building and the residence in the cube above. This cube measures exactly eighteen by eighteen metres and supplies the composition with a stable crown. The living quarters of the governor and family are on top; the general secretary is in the middle; the suite for the guest of honour is underneath. These 'lesser' personages are treated to window embrasures that are slipped subtly off the axis, while the importance of the governor is stressed by the central alignment of his quarters.

Overall, the facade of the Civil Government building tries to unify these disparate elements,

View from entrance hall towards the public square

4. Alejandro de la Sota, 'Anteproyecto para Gobierno Civil en Tarragona', *RNA*, Madrid, May 1957, cited in an unpublished thesis by Joanna Thomas, 'Alejandro de la Sota, Gobierno Civil de Tarragona', Architectural Association Diploma Thesis, 1988.

5. Interview with author, October 1990.

while allowing them to maintain their individual presence. The formal tensions between figure and ground, symmetry and asymmetry, light and shade, axiality and centrifugality, massiveness and transparency, are embedded in the larger theme of an appropriate image for an institution. It is a solution which grapples with a basic dualism in the programme between residential and public functions. De la Sota himself referred to the building in his notes as 'a hierarchical residence (nearly a small palace) ... in which the *balcony* of the governor's office has importance'.[4] The innuendos of authority and participation are played out in contrasts between dense stone surfaces and areas of transparency, while the asymmetrical gestures of the facade hint at lateral or rotational movements in the interiors. Where front and back are accentuated by deep overhangs and plasticity, the sides are detailed to give the sense of a taut surface of stone and glass sheathing. Finally, in the rear facade, the axis of authority is once again stated by means of a huge opening; the motif is recaptured at a smaller scale in the desk of the governor. 'Abstract' de la Sota's building certainly is, but within the abstraction there are numerous subliminal themes relating to the persona of the governor and the rituals of state assembly.

Materials are chosen carefully to underline the idea of an honorific and efficient institution. The external treatment of marble, dark brown bronze, steel and plate glass provides the right note of gravitas while also recalling the seminal

importance of Mies van der Rohe's Barcelona Pavilion in supplying a modern language of a certain opulence and regal character. De la Sota particularly liked to recall that the stone came from local quarries, and that Tarragona is a city dense in Roman memories;[5] in fact, the programme itself insisted upon the use of stone, so the architect needed to find a way of making this material fit with his ideas. The true structure of the Civil Government building is a concrete skeleton with an infill of brick; only the entrance area and the upper terrace in the main facade are treated to steel columns. But through artful detailing, the architect is able to convey the impression of a glass box inserted into a stone sheathing, and to suggest an intermediate zone of ambiguously placed mullions and railings between. The teasing weightlessness of this stone surface is assured by the cantilevers beneath them, by the careful avoidance of vertical alignments, and by the knife-edge device of the two corners which touch, but do not overlap, between levels three and four. The upper portions of the facade read almost as if they had been rent apart, and yet are now being pulled back together by some magnetic force of attraction. The result is an image of considerable tension and mystery that resembles some of Chillida's more haunting sculptures.

One can no doubt make a claim for a Corbusian influence on the Civil Government building. The project would probably have been inconceivable without a thorough knowledge of the villas of the 1920s, the main facade of Garches in particular; and in the stacking up of pieces over a horizontal podium it is possible to catch a faint reminiscence of the project for the Governor's Palace in Chandigarh of 1954. 'Une maison, un palais' – the Tarragona building is clearly both, and resolutely committed to an exploration of the dialectic between the two faces of the governor; public and private. Meanwhile the fusion of features of a palace with the potential of the modern structural frame inevitably recalls the Italian rationalist inheritance (Terragni in particular), while certain details of the ground-level facade – bench, transparent grills, etc. – suggest knowledge of Alvar Aalto's National Pensions Institute in Helsinki of 1948–57.

But the dialogue with tradition is by no means straightforward, as it involves inversions of traditional typologies of civic representation. The idea of 'deconstructing' and reformulating the public palace seems to have been close to de la Sota's intentions from the start. There is an intriguing sheet of sketches which suggests that he was obsessed with the problem. Entitled 'Civil Government – Process of study in the concrete case of Tarragona', this starts by illustrating a 'typical' government building replete with rusticated arcade, *piano nobile*, cornice, flags, shield, etc.[6] It is, in fact, a caricature of the sort of public palace that was still sanctioned and commissioned by the Spanish state as late as the 1950s. Further down the same sheet are doodles of ordinary blocks of flats in several variations, while between the two is a further sketch considering the possibility of a horizontal statement for the main government function. Evidently de la Sota was concerned about how best to combine the residential and symbolic aspects of the programme. The brief for the competition stressed the need to take the building up to a full twenty-one metres, and, given the logic of surface area and access, it followed that one would be forced to somehow combine these disparate functions in a single facade.[7]

De la Sota returns to the problem of hierarchy implicit in such a rationale in the right-hand sequence of sketches. These take the programme of Tarragona and separate them into three main zones divided by open levels of columns. On top is the cube containing 'important residences'; in the middle is the horizontal slab containing the 'government'; in the basement are 'secondary residences' (chauffeurs, maids, etc.). Lower down the same sheet these main elements are combined, then articulated with the help of regulating lines. The main axis is clearly indicated, as is the counterpoint of voids and solids either side. What begins to emerge is a reconstitution of some of the conventional palace 'signs', but within a system of reversals. Where one would expect the solid base there is an open and transparent ground floor; where masonry would be punched with small windows, a transparent skin is masked by floating planes of stone; where the facade would have been continuous, it is here rent asunder into gaping holes. And yet some of the hierarchic qualities and symmetry of the classical palace are retained as an armature and an echo. In the notes accompanying these sketches, de la

Sota states that 'it is a question of hierarchies', and in one doodle even suggests how a bench low down to the right of the entrance may be used to balance a shield far out to the left-hand edge of the first floor.

There is a document dated January 1957 which supplies other insights into de la Sota's interpretation and formal intentions. Entitled 'Anteproyecto para Gobierno Civil en Tarragona', this is written by the architect himself and discusses in detail both the residences and the rationale for their distribution. Towards the end he stresses that he has worked to create a 'facade equilibrium' that is 'dynamic, not static, in character'. He also speaks of his aim of achieving a sober plasticity, including the memorable remark that he has 'struggled with great difficulty to compose a harmonious, hierarchical and noble block': *'un bloque armonioso, jérarquica y noble'*.[8]

The main structural grid of the Civil Government building is laid out on a six-metre interval; in effect, this cuts the building into three lateral bays. The central bay, with its implications of formality, entrance, symmetry, is emphasized at ground level and on the first, second and fifth floors; this works in plan as well as in the main facade. The theme of lateral movement is also articulated through the juxtaposition of partitions, stairs, and structural supports, as in the entrance hall, where the grid can be read both ways: as an entrance portal, or as a ceremonial structure pointing from the lateral benches towards the impressive flight of stairs leading to the piano nobile above. The grid of outer supports coincides with the perimeter of the cube on top, so supplying a very different treatment from the cantilevered overhangs of the main facade. The only firm departure from the module of the concrete skeleton is the row of steel columns in the main facade at ground and terrace levels. These define a gentle curve in plan which picks up the curved boundary of the urban space and which funnels attention towards the main axis. By being recessed more than usual under the slab, these steel columns also dramatize the cantilever and enhance the plasticity of the facade. They give the impression that this is a steel building rather than a concrete one, and they introduce a quiet allusion to a portico of columns. On closer inspection the steel columns reveal themselves to be in a clearly Miesian lineage.

6. 'Gobierno Civil – Proceso para un estudio en el caso concreto de Tarragona': this title appears on the sheet of sketches here illustrated. Original in Fundación Alejandro de la Sota archive.

7. For dimensional constraints of the brief see Thomas, 'Alejandro de la Sota'.

8. All quotations from 'Anteproyecto para Gobierno Civil en Tarragona', dated January 1957; this exists in typescript and in the original pencil draft on trace in the de la Sota archive.

Detail of glass ceiling in entrance hall

9. Navarro Baldeweg, 'Un Laborioso Abstracción'; the English translation of the article appeared in *Architectural Review*, London, May 1986, special editor Peter Buchanan, p. 32 ff.

10. For connections with Mies, interview between author and architect, October 1990, and Alfonso Valdés, 'De Mies van der Rohe a Alejandro de la Sota, o de la grande y honorosa fidelidad a unos principios heredadas', *Arquitectura*, Madrid, November–December 1981; this issue also contains useful articles by Anton Capitel and José Manuel López-Peláez.

11. The phrase is a chapter heading from Le Corbusier, *Vers Une Architecture*, Paris, 1923.

12. See William J. R. Curtis, 'Anatomia de intenciones, El Gimanasio Maravillas', *Arquitectura Viva*, Madrid, November 1988, p. 33 ff; see also José Rafael Moneo in Preface to Harvard exhibition catalogue on de la Sota, Harvard Graduate School of Design, 1987: 'Alejandro de la Sota belongs to a group of architects who, while children of modernity, think that architecture has nothing to do with style.'

13. See note by de la Sota in Harvard exhibition catalogue.

This is but one case of detail being carefully controlled to emphasize the guiding ideas of the building. There are many others – in the jointing of materials, the handling of corners, the slight contrasts in colours of stone, the design of transparent ceilings, furniture, stair rails and the like. De la Sota's method of analysis involved the extensive use of free-hand pencil sketches on thin trace. In these he was able to envision the form and details of his building with considerable accuracy. This design method has been well characterized by Juan Navarro Baldeweg:

'Design always begins with a neat central intuition. The architecture of Alejandro de la Sota – so committed to detail, so tolerant of the fragmentary and the concrete – evolves in a movement from the general to the particular through a series of intellectual transpositions, each extremely carefully elaborated. Such a way of germinating the kernel idea – which remains luminously present as a constant reference throughout the design process – lets it permeate all aspects of the project as an intentional and unifying idea.'[9]

The Civil Government building was a breakthrough. Up to then de la Sota had experimented with several different modes of expression. With the Esquivel Village of two years earlier he had revealed a capacity to manipulate traditional urban typologies in plan, and vernacular references in image. The low-cost housing for Fuencarral B, on the outskirts of Madrid, was an exercise in cut-to-the-bone domestic design for uprooted populations; its atmosphere calls to mind certain neo-realist Italian films of the same period set in the outskirts of industrial cities. The Arvesu house of 1955 was a suave design replete with an undertone of irony and surrealism in some of its details. It was in the TABSA Aeronautical Plant, a project which developed in parallel with the Gobierno Civil, that de la Sota perhaps discovered his pre-disposition for an architectural language rooted in the hard facts of industrial construction. And it was about this time that his obsession with the example of Mies van der Rohe came fully into being.[10]

Mies, for several reasons; first the close connection between idea and technique; secondly, for what de la Sota took to be a sort of 'objectivity' bordering on impersonality; thirdly, for a latent idealism. This transcendental aspect of modern abstraction is crucial in understanding de la Sota's 'sublimation' of the deliberately ordinary and commonplace. He might have endorsed Le Corbusier's definition of architecture as a 'pure creation of the mind'.[11] The 'spiritual' aspects of architecture would not be entirely separable in this instance from a devout Catholicism, just as they would not be with Scarpa, Barragán or Coderch; it may even be that we should here be speaking of a species of 'mystical conservatism'.

After Tarragona, the strategy and the language were more assured and more consistent, but rarely repetitive. To be sure, there were recurrent themes to do with the interplay between the steel skeleton and the wall (whether stone or brick); the direct expression of lighting elements in facade or roof; the unusual use of materials so as to deny conventional expectations about their nature; the search for generators in the forces of climate and terrain, but this was not an architect to hold fast to a priori images. His other major work of the period (I would say his masterpiece), the Maravillas Gymnasium, tells us more about a parallel manner of thinking and a way of feeling than it does about obvious stylistic continuities with Tarragona.[12] The spirit of the method is conveyed well by the architect himself when he says that: 'Themes simplify and offer us possibilities. Architecture does not require that we have recourse to it: it will appear all by itself.'[13]

It was a species of 'functionalism', but one

with a highly intuitive core. Moreover, as the design process of Tarragona suggests, de la Sota's 'purity' and 'distillation' were governed by an inner tension arising from the mastery of polarities. In this case it was a matter of reconciling the architect's modernist ambitions with the monumental conventions of the central government, the planning potential of the concrete skeleton with the requirement to use stone, the dual programmatic demands of public rhetoric and private apartments, the need to project an institution towards the city with the need to retreat behind pockets of shadow for protection from the sun. The object itself is rich in internal dialogues and debates, between massiveness and transparency, symmetry and asymmetry, monumentality and availability. Certain of these inner tensions arise from de la Sota's reading of the specifics of site and programme, others seem to illustrate larger cultural dilemmas of the period. If the struggle between a modernist syntax and a deconstructed image of a public palace addresses the problem of effective state representation, the effort towards fusing abstraction and generic classical values reveals de la Sota's determination to extend certain lines of research in the modern tradition.

It would not be right, then, to isolate this particular solution from recurrent concerns in Spanish modernism such as the transformation of the past, the material expression of ideas, or the poetic response to site and region. Thus the Civil Government building takes its place within a far longer endeavour that goes back to the early 1930s, when architects like José Luis Sert and Josep Torres took account of the pertinent 'Mediterranean' ingredients within the work of the modern masters when formulating a new architecture for Spain, for Catalonia in particular. With the disruption of the Civil War and the ensuing cultural isolationism and conservatism of the 1940s and 1950s, there emerged a strong current of revivalism, returning to revered national icons such as the Escorial for official commissions, and to regional models in the provinces. De la Sota belonged to the generation which came of age in the 1940s and which looked to the exemplars of international modernism as a corrective leading them towards a supposed greater universality.[14] The first cousins of the Civil Government building in Tarragona would seem to be the contemporary

works in and around Barcelona by José Antonio Coderch. These reveal an architecture which is unmistakably modern, and yet which is subtly adjusted to climate and culture; which is directly reliant on structural means yet which has ultimately metaphysical ambitions; which tends towards simplicity and abstraction yet which relies almost unconsciously upon the fund of Spanish tradition.

The Civil Government building crystallizes the social situation which produced it, but it also offers an interesting case of a work which survives a drastic change in political ideology. For, as was mentioned at the outset, this building enjoys a positive reputation in its city and in the retrospective view of younger Spanish designers. An idealist will no doubt affirm that this says something about architectural values 'intrinsic' to the work; a realist might reply that the solution departed enough from the specific conventions of dictatorial expression to allow a shift to new conventions of meaning. It has to be said that this particular break with monumental convention was perhaps possible because of a slight indifference to aesthetic matters on the part of the officials charged with this particular commission.[15] But surely too, all this says something about the capacity of abstraction to generalize a statement so that its 'terms' – entrance, facade, procession, symmetry – may remain, to a degree, non-specific in terms of iconography. Indeed, de la Sota's gestures towards transparency and the melting of the boundary between the institution and the public may have eased the transition towards a democratic use of the building.

But there is something less tangible than this which has to do with the way that new buildings become gradually absorbed into the life and texture of their city. The Civil Government building in Tarragona is a rigorously modern work by the standards of its time, and is nourished by several currents of international architecture, but it is still of its place. Without mimicry of any kind, it manages to distil the identity of a city that has always gained its life from its dual orientation to land and sea. Without excessive gesture or show, it picks up the ancient whispers of an antique Mediterranean town.

14. For the 'generation of the 1940s' see Miguel Angel Baldellou, 'Alejandro de la Sota', Hogar y Arquitectura, November 1974.

15. In interview with author (October, 1990) the architect implied a relative lack of concern with aesthetic matters on the part of his patrons for this commission.

An earlier version of this article appeared in a Festschrift published in honour of Professor Eduard F. Sekler of Harvard University: editor, Wolfgang Böhm, Das Bauwerk und Die Stadt. The Building and the Town. Essays for Eduard F. Sekler, Vienna, 1994, pp. 73–84.

Civil Government building Tarragona 1956–61

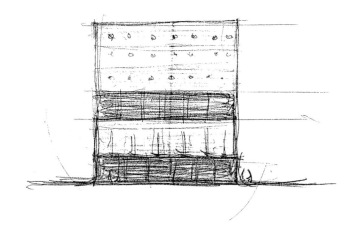

Restored in 1987 by the architect in collaboration with José Llinás

A building representative of the centralized power of Francoist Spain.

A mixed-use programme: official representation, administration, residences. The building can be considered as separate blocks, each corresponding to one of these uses. The representative component has the obligatory axes. The residential block is informal, acting to disrupt the axes. The architecture exploits the differences.

A pristine and well-defined building, based on a six-by-six-metre module. Its clean lines are understood to relate to representation and government.

Everything is made of cut and polished local marble.

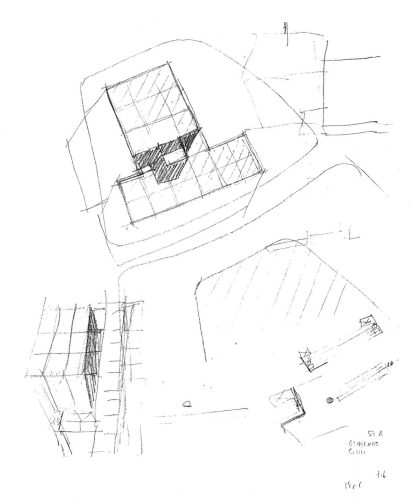

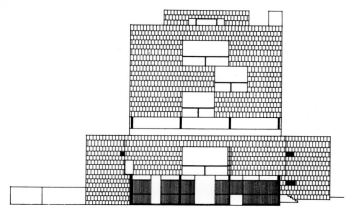

Main elevation

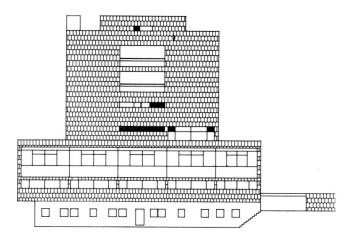

Rear elevation

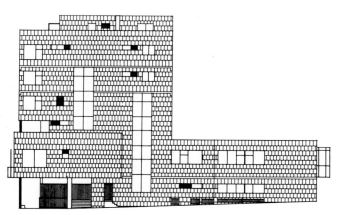

Side elevation

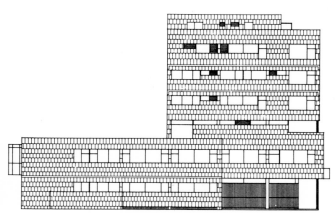

Side elevation

Fifth floor

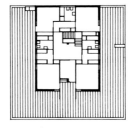

Sixth floor

Third floor

Fourth floor

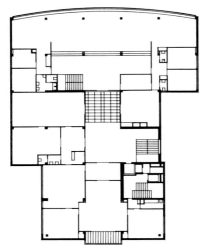

First floor

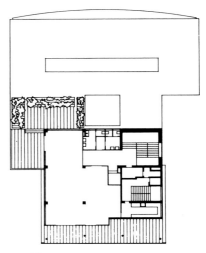

Second floor

Semi-basement

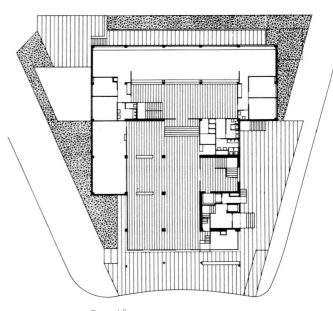

Ground floor

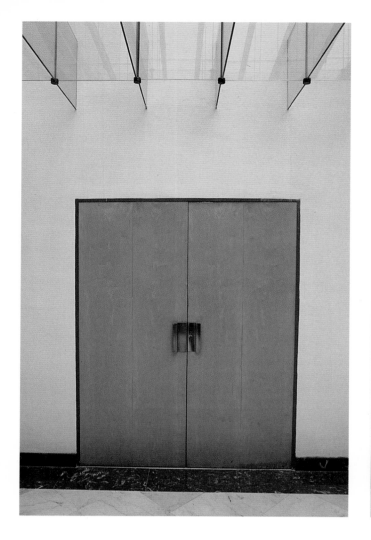
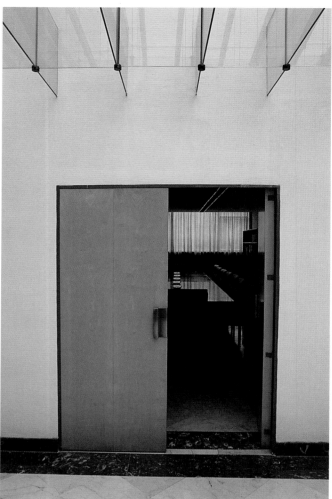

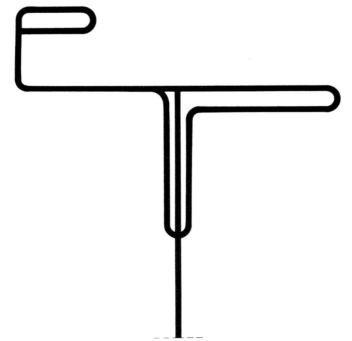

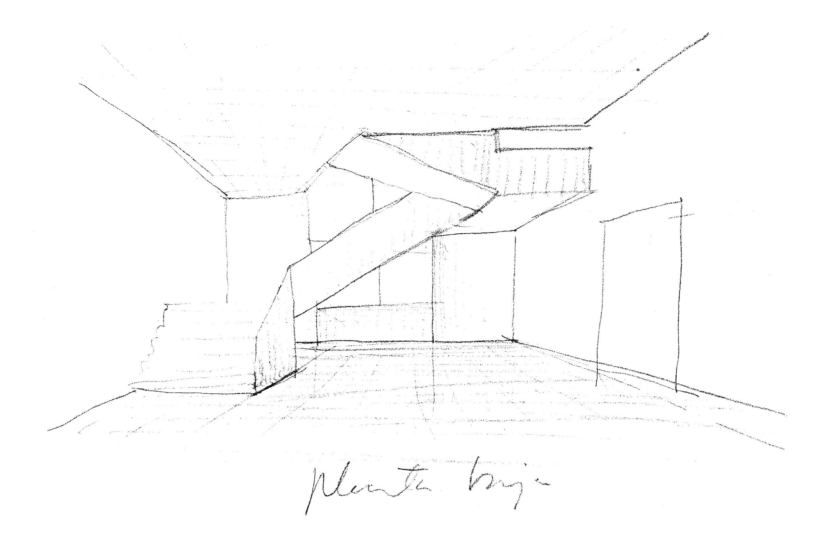

Viewing Sota
Reflections in the Gymnasium

José Manuel López-Peláez

History
A means of entry

At the beginning of the 1960s the Salesian brothers of the Colegio Nuestra Señora de las Maravillas decided to build a multi-use sports hall on the land between the playing-field, which lay in front of their school, and the street at the southern boundary of the site.

The commission to design the Gymnasium was given to Alejandro de la Sota when he was forty-seven years old and had about twenty years of professional experience. A few months before, construction had been completed on the Civil Government building in Tarragona, his prize-winning scheme in a 1957 National Competition. This chronology is important because it relates to a historically significant moment in Spanish architecture: the beginning of a new decade. A general change of direction could be detected: after a slow process of consolidation in the twenty years following the Civil War, modern architecture appeared to have become established. It was also a crucial moment for de la Sota, whose ideas had distilled into a position of clarity and resolution.

For these reasons the Gymnasium project happened at an opportune moment when the place, the brief and de la Sota's own experience could

Site before construction of Gymnasium

work favourably together. Even the *difficulties* of the project became stimuli which served both to reinforce the architect's ideas and strengthen his position.

Not much information remains about the early relationship between de la Sota and the school's board of directors. Nor do we have precise details of the brief. But in general terms the problems to be resolved were quite clear. A contemporary document shows us that the site was trapezoidal in plan and thirty metres wide; it sloped steeply to the southeast, dropping twelve metres in height from the playing-field to the street, which in turn sloped down in an east–west direction. The perimeter to the street was defined by a large niched wall: a *facade* fifty-eight metres long and three storeys high. Thus the building

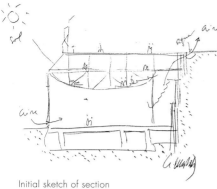

Initial sketch of section

was to be enclosed between the top end of the plot and the two flanking party walls.

The way in which the building is *fitted* into the site is described in the well-known sketch of the section. This drawing explains the *overall concept*, which resolves all of the apparent problems at the same time. De la Sota proposes an initially simple intervention: an extension of the horizontal platform of the existing playing-field over the sloping terrain. At first this seems incomprehensible, in so far as it accentuates the difference in height between the two levels, but it creates a *void* into which the building is inserted. The Gymnasium fills three spatial planes, occupying the whole of the height and expanding horizontally up to the limits defined by the street line and the party walls.

The proposal can be understood as an operation of *completing* the space. The place-making attributes are activated by a series of processes derived from an astute understanding of the *programme*: the retaining wall, inverted trusses with classrooms in their interior, various levels for games, ventilation and natural-lighting systems, etc. are not contrived responses to problems, but rather simple and logical solutions. The building can be conceived of as a *bridge of activities* which is sunk (rooted) in the subsoil and which spans the difference in height between the lowest level of the street and the school's playing-field.

Photographs of the building under construction show twenty-metre tubular inverted trusses supported by simple stanchions, and an innovative cladding being applied to a spectacular skeleton made up of very precise steel sections. These images must have provoked curiosity and astonishment in the people who saw them (it was the first entirely steel frame building in Madrid).

The contrast between the means of construction and the scant technological resources available at that time reveals the *adventurousness* of the construction, as well as the enormous optimism and confidence (de la Sota would say *recklessness*) that animated the design. A parallel can be drawn with works outside Spain which similarly respond to the circumstances of their time, and which make direct use of the material and technical resources of their particular location. One such example might be Stirling and Gowan's Leicester University Engineering Build-

ing, which was also planned in 1960, although it was completed one year after the Gymnasium.

The Maravillas Gymnasium was opened in 1962, and the images of that moment reveal a truly innovatory work. With the passage of time the building has perhaps become even more valued, as a point of reference and place of pilgrimage for successive generations of architects.

Studying the works of Alejandro de la Sota it is possible to discover certain ideas to which he constantly returns: the importance of *functional* layout, clarity of construction, the value of new materials, *lightness*. The Gymnasium became a crucible in which all of these ideas were refined. Both movement through the building and the relations of its various parts are determined, *ineluctably*, by the logic of the programme; each element has its precise location, as in a *puzzle* that is being assembled piece by piece.

The brief asked only for a multi-sports hall, but the proposal incorporated a basement hockey pitch (later converted into a swimming pool), classrooms and other spaces between the trusses, and an extension of the open-air playing-field. The design is not the prescribed result of prevailing conditions but is a *natural* response which generates a credible solution. *New materials* ('Pegaso' sheet metal, 'Viroterm' chipboard, glass of various kinds, etc.) are used not only out of a commitment to the 'spirit of the age' but primarily because they allow an investigation of a new sensibility in which their qualities as *industrial* materials are transformed by their treatment and use. The individuality of the building results from *simple* juxtapositions, reflections, and the precision with which each detail has been formulated.

Arriving at the Gymnasium from the street one must pass obliquely through an iron gate, an entrance seemingly situated almost *by default*, and from this threshold of rather restricted dimensions descend by some steps to another diagonal path which leads to a door whose height is precisely calculated. De la Sota likes the severe proportion of this entrance: 'through a height of 1.9 metres almost everybody passes'. Next the surprise of the interior: a space at the same time both extensive and comprehensible, bathed in light and reflections which change its appearance from one moment to the next. The elements intermingle. Above the basement, which contains the water of

Street facade after restoration (1994)

the swimming pool, are fire from light, earth within the retaining wall, air in every direction, and, most fundamental of all, ether – a *vaporous* atmosphere that is obvious in de la Sota's first sketches of the project, and now perceptible as a physical experience.

The intensity of this interior may distract us from other important themes; for example, the building's sensitive siting and the impression of urban scale that it creates. At the base of the facade, the smooth brick plinth strictly follows the line of the street. At the top, a proportioned relationship of height is established with the adjacent buildings: the Gymnasium continues the cornice of the building on the eastern side, but gradually increases in height as it descends the street. This increase is offset by the planes of glass and projecting glazed bays which punctuate the facade and fragment the volume. Scale, silhouette and materials contribute an urban quality. The

brick and glass both relate the building to the surrounding environment and establish an independent identity; moreover, the point of transition between the two materials is situated approximately at the same height as the wall which existed before the construction of the Gymnasium, as if it were recording traces of a former presence.

The building has two facades. One turns towards the sky: a virtual facade, in the form of the roof, which contains the access from the old part of the school, ventilation grills, water collection devices and glass-block paving. The other facade defines the character and appearance of the building. It consists of a series of superimposed horizontal bands held together by subtle relationships of mathematics and technique, all carefully massed in stable equilibrium on the sloping street. The building projects an appropriate scale, avoiding the unarticulated presence that a sports hall could have produced.

Clockwise from above: the ideas of *repetition*, *flattening/refinement*, *lightness*

Analysis
A game with the Gymnasium

In the Maravillas Gymnasium de la Sota's fundamental ideas are crystallized; it might be suggested that the most deeply held principles of his entire body of work are all precipitated here. By analysing this building in an objective, decontextualized and systematic manner, we may uncover and illuminate these ideas.

The proposed method consists in supposing that the Gymnasium is located in a system of coordinates (as with a geometric function) and investigating what happens in the three spatial planes, on the three axes. To simplify interpretation (an acceptable move in a *scientific* game) these will be considered independently of one another.

The longitudinal direction (*x axis*) contains the idea of *repetition*. The proposal is based on a structural sequence formed by the twenty-metre-wide trusses set at right angles to the street and repeated on a six-metre interval. If this module were carried through, it would exceed the dimension of the site and would also make it regular. This is evident at the juncture between the trusses and the party wall on the west side, where the structure remains parallel without revealing the oblique angle of the boundary.

De la Sota would have preferred that the trapezoidal site were rectangular, and in fact he tried to negotiate the exchange of a strip of land on the west side, which ultimately he was unable to acquire. Thus, the small road provided at this location has a dual purpose, not only allowing direct access from the street to the basement, but also compensating for the irregularity of the interior space.

When de la Sota comments on this point he usually refers to the popularity of the contrary approach, which gives importance to geometric complexity; he speaks with irony of the compulsion to employ (pointlessly) elaborate methods and jokes about the 'inspiration' that some architects have found in the oblique line that was imposed on him here.

In the Gymnasium this idea of *repetition* is fundamental in understanding the upper storey, where the module is used as an ordering mechanism, as a spatial discipline. In this way, any singularity that deviates from the norm only serves to reinforce its precise nature.

Related to the idea of *repetition* are those of *simplicity* and spatial *unity*, both particularly important for Alejandro de la Sota. These combine to form '*the world in a grid*' – a Cartesian totality implying the use of a few elements which acquire intensity in their paucity; or the presence of a thread of affinity which relates some parts to others, as happens on the facade where the repeated module of fenestration gives dimension to the assembly, the projecting glazed bays, and the evenly spaced trusses that crown the building. De la Sota talks of the necessity for self-discipline: the line which divides the two textures of the brick plinth is, he says, 'the only capricious line of the Gymnasium' – it sets up a vibration as if 'in a Bach partita'.

Also related to *repetition* are the ideas of *modulation* and *regularity*, which are seen as instruments necessary to obtain clarity of function and technique; from that *modern* attitude also proceeds the desire for mass production and industrialization. A precise module and carefully controlled tolerances enable elements to be fabricated in the workshop and adjusted on site: this is a *physical* architecture of juxtaposed but still recognizably distinct pieces, as opposed to a *chemical* architecture, formed by parts which 'react' with each other and lose their individual identity.

The view along the longitudinal axis of the Gymnasium reveals a sense of motion which, definitively, has to do with the idea of *repetition*. Thus, the entrance is not frontal but is produced as a deviation from the linear; and all of the principal systems of movement through the building follow this same line. Moreover, when de la Sota shows exterior photographs of the Gymnasium he prefers oblique views, or else frontal images including moving cars – streaks on the exterior which reproduce the movement in the interior, from one end of the games court to the other.

Next we look at the Gymnasium from the cross axis (*y axis*): in the sense of its depth. The plans and cross sections come into play now, as they illustrate most clearly the decision to 'control' the space between the plane defined by the street and the retaining wall at the top end of the site. This intervention implies a spatial *compression* which, ultimately, is transmitted to all parts of the building, even to the very material from which it is constructed. The result of such compression is *flatness*. In keeping with this idea, the materials tend to display the minimum possible thickness. The desired appearance is one of smoothness, as if each of the parts were being condensed into an ideal plane.

An examination of the cross section reveals

Archive photograph of sports hall

that the 'convexity' of the inverted trusses could be interpreted not so much as an expression of load-bearing but rather as a distortion produced by the horizontal compression forces at their ends. This same pressure appears to bear down on the raked seating, exaggerating its pitch and gradually compressing it against the retaining wall, the upper part of which vibrates as it allows the 'air' produced by this force to escape. It is the same 'air' which is depicted in the initial sketch showing the cross ventilation of the building, and which, as *ether*, creates an 'atmosphere' within the interior of the Gymnasium that is paradoxically both vaporous and taut at the same time.

If one were to employ this same approach in looking at the plan of the Gymnasium one might think that perhaps the site was not initially trapezoidal, but rather rectangular, and that the oblique shape had been produced by the same effect of lateral compression, by a 'slippage' between the different ideal lines of the plan. Such a slippage would have produced a similar obliquity in the party walls and a greater proximity between the facade and the retaining wall.

The idea of *flatness* has to do with the *refined treatment* of materials and details, and is expressed as much in de la Sota's way of drawing as it is in his approach to construction. The steel sections become dividing lines which fragment surfaces (for example, in the roof of the sports hall or in the articulation of the joinery). Surfaces also 'dematerialize', as happens with the wire safety fence; or form virtual planes, as is the case with the series of ridges which carry the upper edge of the skylights.

But it is important to understand how much this lateral *pressure* causes a range of elements to vibrate, never allowing them to assume a position of equilibrium. For example, the corrugated metal in the projecting bays, the pitch of the skylights, and the diagonal bracings in the rooftop safety fence all suggest the presence of an *immaterial* ideal plane in which the whole of the Gymnasium facade becomes condensed. On examination of the two textures which form the brick plinth, one notices that the smooth upper part is recessed slightly in relation to the rougher lower part, demonstrating the 'effort' required for fashioning a plane – an 'impossible' plane, which is expressed by its absence. This tension abates, as

Projecting bays of Gymnasium after restoration (1994)

flatness, possible only at the ends, is produced in a literal form.

Related to the adjustment of the thickness of material is the idea of *lightness*, although that idea acquires its principal sense in the vertical axis of the Gymnasium: the *z axis*. The desire for the building to weigh as little as possible results in a strategy to counter the force of gravity, which is reflected, above all, in the elevation and sections of the building. The question that de la Sota posed is well known: 'How much does a building weigh?'. Equally famous is his answer: 'A heavy building? I don't know how to make one...' In both one detects his conviction that light material is more potent than dense.

In the Gymnasium the dominance of the *light* object is firmly established, not only in the use of lightweight materials: steel sections, corrugated metal, glass, wood, etc., but also in the manner of arranging them. The large inverted trusses appear to hang in the glass, they are 'suspended' in *light* and *reflections*, essential components of lightweight material. Even the brick, a dense material, is used as if it weighed nothing. Looking up the facade one observes that the brick plinth does not touch the floor: it 'hovers' in the *air*. Higher up, the facade is made of glass which folds backwards and extends into a *halo* (composed of the trusses, safety barriers and wire fence), which dissolves the building in the *air*.

If we now recall the way of entering the Gymnasium from the street we can verify that the effect of vertical compression on the entrance contrasts with the experience of the expansion of the interior space, and that both are functions of the z axis. Now we can feel the rising air that was drawn in the initial sketch, and perceive it as a force capable of keeping the roof *afloat*. That force is apparent in the subtle atmosphere which pervades all of this great space.

An upward passage through the interior carries us on a journey, which overcomes gravitational pull, towards the roof, the *open air* of the other playing-field. The journey can also be made in reverse, from the highest level down to the street, by way of the *air-to-air* bridge that the Gymnasium forms. In both directions ascending air and gravity are counterpoised forces which tend to balance out the sensation of movement.

Epilogue
Provisional, after a visit

The ideas that have been set out address some of the issues which emerge from a study of the Gymnasium and other buildings by de la Sota.

The first issue has to do with the category of *perfection*. The work of de la Sota was compared at one time to that of Mies, and, without doubt, that architect is very important to him. But they differ in their ideas of perfection. In the Gymnasium *perfection* is present in the ideas of *refinement*, *regularity* and *modulation*, which have already been mentioned: however, de la Sota believes that architecture must not be completely resolved, but rather find that point at which it gains in vitality; it is necessary to know when to stop refining the detailing, so as to preserve the tension of the work as a whole. De la Sota says that architecture must have a certain *deshabillé* or unmasked quality. This proposition distances him from 'high-tech', and establishes a link with Le Corbusier which initially would not be so obvious.

A second issue is connected to the very content of the Gymnasium: *games*, considered not in relation to the character of the building but as part of the very process which drives the proposal. It has been said that the Gymnasium represents an optimistic moment in the work of Don Alejandro, but this happiness arises from the architect's approach to the problem. De la Sota's rigour does not override his *sense of humour*, which allows him to turn things around and present ideas which might seem preposterous on first sight. The happiness brought to his work is transformed into *freshness*, and in this is rooted a large part of its attraction. This also provides a point of interest for present-day students of architecture who are subjected to the task of design. Don Alejandro affirms: 'I have never laughed more than in front of the drawing board'; that laugh is later transformed into an imperceptible smile before the astonished look of his interlocutor.

The final issue refers to a consideration of the temporal, not in the historical sense but rather in what is referred to as the *durability* of buildings. De la Sota states that modern architecture has to bequeath *ideas* rather than *traces* to the future, and also that it is an architecture especially affected by the apathy of society. He asserts, in the same way, that it cannot age with *honourable wounds* like architecture built in stone, but may, very easily, when cleaned and restored, regain its *youth* and *freshness*. The Gymnasium has been used extensively for many years and has resisted *old age* better than many modern works, although it has endured alterations and the deterioration of part of its fabric. (De la Sota says: 'Bodies deteriorate; look at Greta Garbo!')

Don Alejandro referred to the *age* of the Gymnasium in an exhibition of his drawings which opened in the CRC Gallery in Barcelona in May 1985, shortly before the facade of the building was restored for the first time. For this occasion he prepared a text which reads thus:

'The Maravillas Gymnasium is already twenty-two years old. I don't know why I made it as I did, but what I do know is that I am not displeased with the outcome.

'I believe that one way of making Architecture is *not* to make it, and that, by *not* making Architecture, we do it a greater service than those who continually apply their *knowledge* to it.

'A problem was solved then, and the solution still works today, and it seems to me that nobody misses the Architecture that is not there.'

In 1994 I visited the Gymnasium again. Under de la Sota's control, the building was being restored once more, and the work extended from the facade to certain areas of the interior. Some rooms had been dismantled (*physical architecture*) and part of the uncovered structure had been revealed, exposing raw nerves and evoking the time, at the beginning of the 1960s, when the Gymnasium was under construction.

The metal fittings were being replaced with others of a very precise modern design, steel was giving way to lacquered aluminium, and the junctions between pieces, made by hand in the original, were being replaced with items of modern technology.

The building had lost something of its *deshabillé* quality and was acquiring a more technically polished image. Fresh paintwork and different colour schemes had given it a renewed presence.

De la Sota has commented to me: 'The Gymnasium resists a lot'. It may also resist *perfection*.

This is a revised and expanded version of an article which appeared in Spanish in *Anales de Arquitectura*, University of Valladolid, no. 6, 1995.

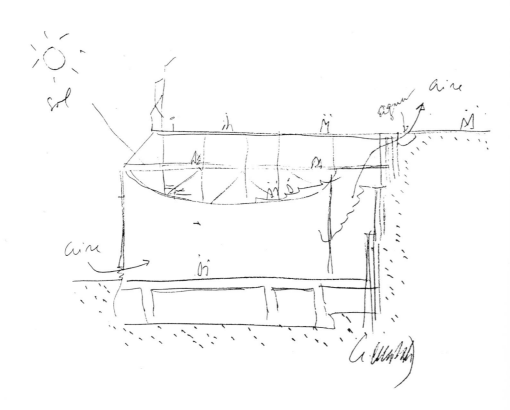

Engineer: Eusebio Rojas Marcos

This building arose almost out of the air. Our preoccupation with the problems of the urban context, the difficult site and the budget left no leeway for making decisions about the Architecture, which is perhaps why it has no Architecture at all.

I don't know why I made it as I did, but what I do know is that I am not displeased with the outcome.

I believe that one way of making Architecture is not to make it, and that, by not making Architecture, we do it a greater service than those who continually apply their *knowledge* to it.

A problem was solved then, and the solution still works today, and it seems to me that nobody misses the Architecture that is not there.

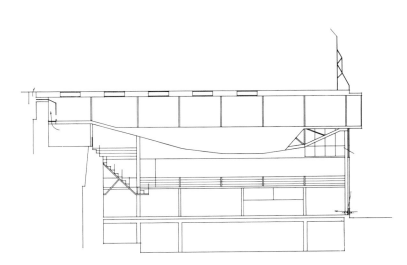

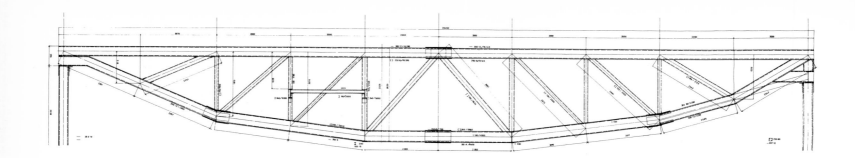

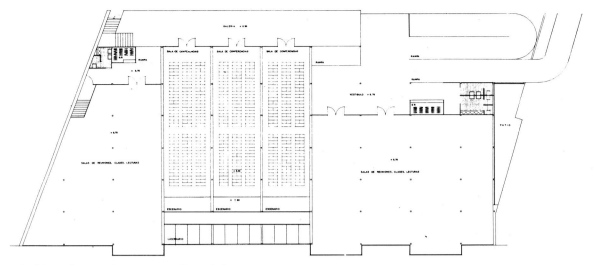

Third floor: classrooms between trusses; lecture halls

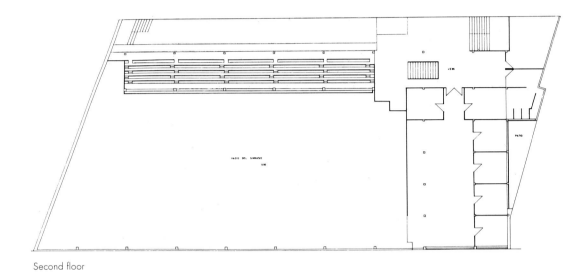

Second floor

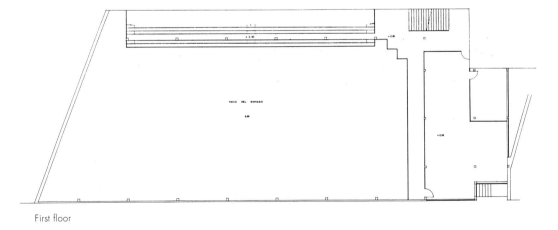

First floor

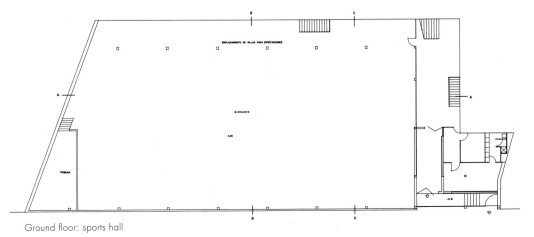

Ground floor: sports hall

Alejandro de la Sota:
the construction of an architect

Iñaki Abalos

Left: Post Office and Telecommunications building, León

Just at the moment when Alejandro de la Sota's career was becoming established, he decided to stop and take stock of what it was that he really wanted to do and, more importantly, who he wanted to be. For the next two years he withdrew from his usual preoccupations and started the task that would take him the rest of his life: self-creation, the construction of a unique creative persona, the transformation of his career into the most ardently pursued project in his office: *the construction of a new concept of the architect.* This period of detachment was not merely a personal gesture – the phrase 'to stand back in order to see more clearly' expresses the etymological origin of the word 'theory', and it is from this perspective that de la Sota's creation of an 'I' different from all other 'I's can best be understood. At this time in his life he had proved himself an equal amongst his peers, but he aspired to something else, to a state perhaps best described by Blake: 'I must Create a System, or be enslav'd by another Man's. I will not Reason and Compare; my business is to Create.'

So, what image of the architect did Alejandro de la Sota create? Despite (or because of) the political situation in Spain – a lengthy dictatorship, violent at first, then sad and bureaucratic – he became an architect who was illuminated by the present, in constant dialogue with the global

reality that others failed to perceive; an architect who attempted to articulate his thoughts and actions in a manner both pragmatic and critical, who looked for ways to work within the methods of material production without either being subsumed into or marginalized by the system. And in so doing he defended the profession's peculiar historical description of itself as a socially desirable, artistic practice while giving it new content and programmes. This interest in both theoretical and practical issues – and the ability to synthesize them – places his work in opposition to the growing tendency towards specialization, towards a greater division between the roles of technician, creator, and teacher. For de la Sota these elements co-exist and support each other. Thus, he can be situated in a tradition similar to that of contemporary neo-pragmatism, as exemplified in the writings of Richard Rorty. Indeed, the parallels are so striking that his work might be suspected of following Rorty's thinking instead of preceding it.

The following discussion attempts to describe this hypothetical Sotaean project of self-creation, to reveal and explain the ways and means of constructing a new definition of the contemporary architect. We will seek a record of this 'construction', an explanation of the techniques that form this definition, and an instruction manual indicating how these may be assembled to form a

53

the contemporary world and the modern masters the very techniques he had extracted from them, thereby establishing a distance which in turn opened the way for the creation of a new system. Modernism and America at first appeared to him to be the sources of this assembling technique:

As luck would have it, I thought that this was a path which led towards an inevitable, imminent end. I believe that you should not do what you know how to do, but should always expose yourself to new things, remembering what you've done before. I faced a terrible loss of confidence as the path turned out to be leading nowhere. I was not having fun any more, and I spent several years without working.

While in this state of 'to be or not to be', I chanced upon a book of the work that Gropius and Breuer had built after they reached the United States. I saw clearly how they had arrived at an Architecture which I would call physical, by which I mean that it has the quality of uniting opposing elements so as to create a third element, which, without losing any of the properties of its constituents, contains some absolutely new ones of its own.

The Maravillas, Miraflores and Tarragona projects are exemplars of this technique of 1 + 1 = 3, of de la Sota's interest in joining things and making them speak, both individually and together. But this method achieved its full potential only in the 1970s, when he began to apply it to the modern masters, relating their teachings to architecture's ideological crisis so as to open up a conversation in which the conceptual foundation of modernism was overlaid with other concerns. He raised the level of dialogue – which up to then had been based on the material, the 'physical' – by introducing elements that were spiritual or related to temporal concerns.

This 'system' took its place within a conception of the present that speaks to us directly, describing our world appositely and accurately. It was de la Sota's very admiration for the modernists which allowed him to place them in their historical context, opening up a dialogue in which they could be considered from a different perspective and in relation to different themes. Out of this displacement, the system of Alejandro de la Sota gained its definitive form.

From above: Esquivel Village, 1955;
Children's summer home, Miraflores, 1957;
César Carlos hall of residence, 1967

De la Sota and the techniques of time: contingency

For the modernists time ran into the future. Imbued with faith in progress, they were motivated by an unshakeable belief in modern technology and its capacity to bring happiness to a cohesive, compact society based on the figure of the male and his model Calvinist family. The future was always to be preferred to the past, the visible to the hidden, the logical to the irrational, the industrial to the manual: the air became clinical and space lost its density as everything was transformed into an all-embracing panopticon.

But after Hiroshima, belief in technology foundered and time began to run backwards. Now suffused with an impossible nostalgia for an original state of grace, and motivated by the desire to establish a non-destructive relationship with nature, architecture devolved a creative role to the individual. In place of the material, didactic character of the collective project came something more anarchistic, focused on private expression. The past became the model for the present; the dark, the hidden, and the fragmentary came to be seen as more fertile sources of inspiration than the light, the visible, and the unitary.

There was, so to speak, both a teleological time, which was projected into the future and which found its justification in positivism and in public culture; and a genealogical time, beginning with the past, in which there was a recovery of existential, individual expression – of the right to difference.

But although these ideas undoubtedly stimulated the appearance of alternative ideals in architecture, there are other conceptions of time whose importance should not be underestimated. For example, it would be difficult to understand Mies van der Rohe, who was de la Sota's greatest inspiration, without taking into account Nietzsche's theory of time as a cycle – an 'eternal return' – which greatly influenced Mies and many of his contemporaries in Germany, including Taut and the 'Expressionist Brotherhood'. Nietzsche's idea of the relation between memory and the future was very different from the sentiments of the positivists or the later nostalgia of the Heideggerians. Much of this is reflected in de la Sota, in his great affinity with Mies, in his first, rather expressionist projects, or indeed in his decision to construct himself as an artist.

But there is something which distinguishes de la Sota from many of the modernists, postmodernists and expressionists who have attempted to give form to the passage of time. It is his balanced approach: his capacity to acknowledge the subjectivity of the idea of time and the pragmatic value of being aware of its multiplicity and contingency while remaining certain that the present has an active role to play as the place of experimentation and the arbiter of the multiple arrows of time that pierce it.

De la Sota uses time as a spatial technique to activate air and make it 'converse' – and this is a key term in pragmatic techniques, a kind of metatechnique which serves to define the material and constructive aspects of architecture.

It is this which permits multiple strands of inquiry and opposites to co-exist and not lapse into either incompatibility or eclecticism but produce the studied ambiguity that is characteristic of de la Sota's work: a paradoxical and elegant effect that recognizes our inherent multiplicity. Like a mannerist Saint Sebastian, the Sotaean architect feels not despair but pleasure in being pierced by the arrows of time. Tarragona, Salamanca, Miraflores, León, Esquivel, Cesar Carlos and Alcudia are all works in which the present acquires brilliance as a point of intersection, a product of the combination of counterpoised vectors, a pure expression of our multiplicity.

De la Sota and material techniques: solidarity

What lies behind de la Sota's insistence on the constructive aspects of the discipline? His dedication has often been interpreted as a modernist's 'act of resistance', more out of a lack of critical resources than out of conviction. Certainly, he had faith in industrial techniques at a time when technology and industry were anathema. But, more than that, he took obvious delight in using these techniques to confer an elegance upon the process of construction. Where before there was the emotion elicited by the epic dimension of the work, there now appeared the pleasure of ease, the replacing of physical effort with intellectual effort, the effacing of all nostalgia, no matter how

Post Office and Telecommunications building, León: detail of facade

well masked, for the heavy labour of slaves. The derogatory 'too easy' gave way to the derogatory 'too difficult', the muscular jump of the athlete to the agile flight of the ballerina.

The pragmatic architect is above all the one who gives a hearing to the conventional and the banal, the one who respects the poetic dimension of the here and now, the one who is able to take familiar things out of their usual context and give them the brilliance of poetry. It is from this viewpoint that we should evaluate de la Sota's insistence on the elements of construction. He showed us that we may transcend the discipline, not by abandoning its more routine components, but rather by recognizing in them the full poetic force of an original act. This belief requires the architect to reach a compromise with society: an attitude far removed from the social messianism of modernism. Basic decisions affect the whole process of construction and everyone involved in it. The appearance of ease, the down-playing of the architect's role, has therefore to be reflected in something more than the clean details favoured by minimalists. What de la Sota advocates is not so much cleanness as simplicity, a conservation of effort, a further easing of the process as a whole. The time of construction is also, for de la Sota, a time for consolidation, for making everything as painless as possible. Pragmatists have no fundamental truths to defend, nothing to sacrifice in the name of originality or the final result. But rather, by minimizing all difficulties, they establish a way

of working that is both effective and progressive, and which implies a new aesthetic.

The work is not about 'invention' – the concept of the architect as an artisan initiated into the mysteries of the process; it is about 'intention' – about collecting the things produced by society and re-directing them towards new and unusual applications, thereby both restoring a critical dimension to the making of architecture and re-establishing a dialogue with the present, with the here and now, with what exists and ought to be looked at as something capable of creating emotion and beauty.

There is no attempt to acquire an exhaustive knowledge of matters outside the discipline: the pragmatic builder does not get caught up in details; he doesn't need them, for he is capable of reducing the process of construction to a few, simple operations of assembling compatible sub-systems. The initial paradox of de la Sota's buildings – the fact that details are practically non-existent – provides the key to understanding the importance in pragmatic thought of the idea of 'system'. In this perspective, the traditional idea of the builder is replaced with the idea of a creator of systems – of groups of elements that are capable of establishing a logical internal order but also of keeping this order sufficiently open to accommodate surprise and contradiction. Like the rules of a game, a good system can be gauged in terms not only of its economy but also of its indeterminacy: the degree of openness it allows. Thus, creative development evolves from the game.

If we now return to the projects in Alcudia and León, pausing this time to look at the material rather than the temporal techniques, it becomes clear that both projects are defined by the same system. This system is in turn defined by a small number of appropriate components specified from manufacturers' catalogues. These components were designed for industrial and/or commercial construction: lightweight composite cladding panels, corrugated steel sheet, standard prefabricated partitions and finishes, exposed fittings, etc. But here they have been translated to a housing complex and a public building and endowed, respectively, with a domesticity and a monumentality which cast them in a new light.

In both projects the act of construction has

only two moments: the preparation of the site and the in-situ assembly of components prefabricated off site and delivered by lorry. But in each case this easy, light system is used to create a very different image. The public building simulates solidity, appearing to be wrapped in heavy boulders, whereas the traditional housing scheme feigns a contradictory stability with its factory-made, transportable parts. The monumentality of León and the privacy of Alcudia are both achieved with a material the width of a cigarette paper: five centimetres of polyurethane. Here in the material techniques we again find ambiguity and multiplicity of meaning, a need to express the fragility of our existence as well as the value of memory – and a delight in the efficiency of working with lightweight building systems

The process of construction with lightweight techniques gives rise to a phenomenology of immateriality. Or, to be more precise, almost-immateriality, because it is in this 'almost' that we may find the link between architecture – the construction of real physical experiences – and contemporary technological developments, which de la Sota's work shows can be codified within the discipline of architecture. As he put it, in one of his paradoxical aphorisms, it is a matter of achieving 'as much nothing as possible' – a summation of an ironic pragmatic manifesto on the use of material techniques.

De la Sota and rhetorical techniques: irony

In constructing his project of a new contemporary architect de la Sota acquired an extraordinary awareness of the range of techniques – subjective and objective, temporal and material – that had to be applied simultaneously to prevent architecture from lapsing into its reductivist incarnations: the building and the manifesto. The examples of Alcudia and León allow us to interpret his earlier works as steps that brought him closer towards a complete system, towards his self-creation as an artist. But this description of the system underlying the creation of a new image of the architect is not yet complete, for an architect, more than someone who merely builds, is also someone who constructs fantasies and illusions using images and words: someone who draws,

a maker of plans, as well as someone who describes and instructs, who uses words as a complement to the system. The final step is to develop the necessary techniques of persuasion, for we find it hard to accept that an architect is new if he persists in using old vocabularies and techniques in his drawn or written documents; if he is unable to re-describe these and make them interact with the present time and context.

We have to remember that few people owe a greater debt to rhetoric than do the pragmatists, who take up their role as opponents of the metaphysical tradition, following the sophists (the first rhetoricians), the nominalists (the inheritors of medieval rhetoric), and Nietzsche. From their perspective, the first requirement of rhetoric is not rationality or the logical validation of the discourse, but the pure creation of the effect of truth, persuasion, a re-description of reality using new metaphors that are capable of explaining the world in more credible way: hence the technique of the aphorism, the proposal of an alternative truth which dispenses with demonstrations and syllogisms.

De la Sota, along with a small number of his contemporaries, was aware of the importance of techniques of persuasion, of rhetoric, as a component of the system, to be applied neither before nor after the other techniques but simultaneously and in conjunction with them. Thus we begin to realize the close relation that exists between his aphoristic texts, his synthesizing drawings, and the series of actions described above.

It is de la Sota's own words that give the clearest indication of how little his theoretical activity has to do with a search for certainties: we find only radical redescriptions of apparently neutral and unproblematic phenomena; paradoxes; new metaphors. As with Nietzsche, de la Sota's most successful writings are infused with a picaresque spirit, like that of a mischievous child. His explanations are given force by his use of vivid imagery and his ability to surprise: the descriptive moment (a memory of the project) is never split from the proposition (a theoretical writing): instead each is interwoven with the other: the descriptions are re-descriptions, and the re-descriptions are proposals framed in the rhetorical technique of Sotaean aphorisms.

It is now the moment to re-visit Alcudia and

León, guided only by de la Sota's texts – his memories of the project – and his drawings, both sketches and technical drawings, which reveal his evocative powers, his irony, his aphoristic, persuasive syncretism. This is how he explains the Alcudia project:

Man is by nature territorial. Traditionally, if the climate was propitious, he needed only to mark his territory superficially, in the manner of the lion's roar, the fox's scent. But if he wished to satisfy his innate desire for privacy, he had to have a sheltered place to work and rest. By making his home an enclosure, Man attained all this, but lost Nature. So he looked for a way to recover it – if not wholly, at least in part.

Thus the courtyard was invented. The courtyard can be found everywhere, from Pompeii through to Mies, and not least of all in Spain: it is set inside the house, if space permits; if not, it is adjacent, contiguous and defined by walls.

The desire to possess nature is so notoriously widespread that there is nothing more characteristic of the landscape than the rural wall. Miles and miles of walls have found their way on to the finest canvases.

The intention here was to make an urban housing development with additional walls, which afford more privacy. The space inside is covered with vines, climbing plants and awnings. In this way the small plot of land acquires the character of a grand habitation.

We will live under pergolas built by the vines. Who doesn't have a memory of the huts of road-workers or level-crossing guards?

The shaded terrace also acts as a 'periscope', giving each house distant views of the mountains and the sea. A small pool of sea water is added too.

All of the construction is prefabricated and transported complete from the factory to where ever, in this case to Mallorca. Sheet metal panels and partitions, forged sheet metal, fittings made in the workshop, large blocks of prefabricated paving, all easily assembled. This saves time, assures quality, and gives rise to forms which are sometimes far removed from architecture.

To see the sea from all of these houses; to live intimately in all of them.

The idea was to make the house open, turning the plot, the garden, into part of the house, covering it with bougainvillaea, climbers... And above the plants, the observatory-solarium.

And this is what he wrote about León:

It is said that Le Corbusier, on returning from his first trip to New York, wrote to the city's mayor: 'Demolish New York, and I will build you a cube that works.' The story may be true, or apocryphal; in either case it has had a serious impact on architects who have heard it. It inspired a phase of form-giving in which the various parts of a programme of requirements were massed together in *volumetric compositions*.

'A cube that works' weighs a lot...

These things can be seen as indications of approaching change: instead of being restricted by scale we can proceed to work on all scales.

Before beginning the design we have to take account of the possibilities offered by today's new means of construction. The legacy of the past tends to be overvalued; nostalgia has combined with fear to establish the idea that it is better to restore than to build anew. But this is not so. It all depends on our approach to the task of design.

Paul Klee said, 'We do not yet have the strength for the final endeavour because we do not have the masses on our side...'

The Post Office and Telecommunications building in Léon is a 'functional' building, made with state-of-the-art technology. Possibly this is all it is. The idea was to make a 'cube that works' and is adaptable to future changes in use. This flexibility is achieved by the simplification of the structure and the clarity of the interior. Clarity! Light, and more light!

Care has been taken to provide this calm parallelepiped with the prestigious touches appropriate to a public building.

The endeavour to locate new materials continues apace. In León we have used Robertson panels, which are usually found in supermarket construction. Their application here, to a quite singular, important building, has achieved a perfectly acceptable result, which offends no one's sensibilities. This is because the panes have been painted on the exterior to approximate the typical 'León' [also Spanish for 'lion'] colour and tone, whilst in the interior they have been given a delicate 'human' touch.

These texts provide a clear statement of the pragmatic architect's fusion of the roles of critic, teacher, technician, and creator. They also show how finely disguised humour, irony – the rhetorical term for expressing the opposite of what you say – is not simply a distinguishing trait of the author but an integral part of the 'system', the thing that makes it possible for opposites to co-exist, the unguent that smoothes the way for the creation of a new unifying identity.

The same irony, with the same synthesizing properties, can be found in the drawings that de la Sota made after his second period of contemplation at the beginning of the 1970s – a period during which he developed the refining technique that came to characterize all his subsequent work. In earlier works such as Tarragona the representation is effective but conventional: the walls are given thickness and the lines, including those of the sections and perspectives, emphasize certain aspects of the building's solidity; the drawings serve above all to describe a physical reality. In the Post Office and Telecommunications building in León and in the offices for Aviaco, however, the drawing rebounds, like an echo or reflection of the architecture: systematic, diagrammatic, the plans no longer attempt to present physical attributes but can be read as plans for assembling the parts of the system, and also as rhetorical demonstrations of the simplicity of this constructive approach – the need solely for a schematic representation – and of the type of beauty that can result. Details simply vanish after 1967, when a monograph personally supervised by de la Sota deprived readers of the opportunity of seeing a single construction detail. In this apparent state of asepsis, he took calligraphy as a model to evoke the dematerialization and simplicity that he sought, as well as the aesthetic of 'as much nothing as possible' that permeated the work as a whole. These drawings show the search for and iden-

tification of a system as being of primary importance to de la Sota. They represent the simultaneous materiality and immateriality of the system: each line refers to a different piece, all the lines are equal – in the system there are no hierarchies, each link has equal importance. The drawings have no details because the system resists particularization. It is this omission which gives the system its perfection and its breadth.

During this period there was also an increased use of free-hand sketches to accompany descriptions that became less material and more atmospheric, reflecting an almost naive contentment. Others have discussed the ways in which de la Sota's penchant for caricature, for reducing everything to a few exaggerated strokes, is related to his means of evoking architecture (in León, for example), being part of a good-humoured process of simplification. There is a certain mischief or irony in his view of his own work, but also a private acceptance that the 'system' leads to a clarity which allows him to escape a world defined by Great Truths and gain a foothold in a more fragile sphere, in the fleeting instant, in the innocent pleasures of simplicity and humour.

There is something very appealing about this Sotaean project of self-creation, about the way in which he developed it throughout an extended period (though perhaps not with the self-awareness described here), finally arriving at a prototype of the contemporary architect: himself. Despite some major setbacks the outcome was always clear: the attainment of that private happiness implied in the quotation from Blake which began this simulated technical memory. That is itself also a re-description whose single theme is not so much historical truth – what can this be? – as an invitation to create truth: 'I must Create a System, or be enslav'd by another Man's. I will not Reason and Compare; my business is to Create.'

Note. This article has in a large part been inspired by Richard Rorty's book, *Contingency, Irony, and Solidarity*, Cambridge University Press, 1989, which has served to illuminate an image of Alejandro de la Sota that is so often obscured by its own brilliance, and to give unity and identity to its various manifestations. I have also been helped and informed by numerous articles written by various authors, and, more particularly, by conversations with Alejandro de la Sota and with Juan Herreros.

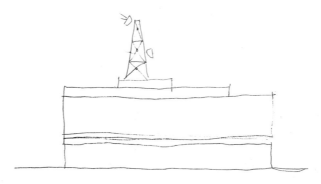

It is said that Le Corbusier, on returning from his first trip to New York, wrote to the city's mayor: 'Demolish New York, and I will build you a cube that works.'

The story may be true, or apocryphal; in either case it has had a serious impact on architects who have heard it.

It inspired a phase of form-giving in which the various parts of a single programme of require-ments were massed together in *volumetric compositions.*

'A cube that works' weighs a lot.

These things can be seen as indications of approaching change: instead of being restricted by scale, we can proceed to work on all scales.

Before beginning the design we have to take account of the possibilities offered by today's new means of construction. The legacy of the past tends to be overvalued; nostalgia has combined with fear to establish the idea that it is better to restore than to build anew. But this is not so. It all depends on our approach to the task of design.

Paul Klee said, 'We do not yet have the strength for the final endeavour, because we do not have the masses on our side...'

The Post Office and Telecommunications Building in León is a 'functional' building, made with state-of-the-art technology. Possibly this is all it is. The idea was to make a 'cube that works', and is adaptable to future changes in use. This flexibility is achieved by the simplification of the structure and the clarity of the interior. Clarity! Light, and more light!

Care has been taken to provide this calm parallelepiped with the prestigious touches appropriate to a public building.

The search for new materials continues apace. In León we have used Robertson panels, which are usually found in supermarket construction. Their application here, to a quite singular, important building, has achieved a perfectly acceptable result, which offends no one's sensibilities. This is because the panels have been painted on the exterior to approximate the typical 'León' colour and tone, whilst in the interior they have been given a delicate 'human' touch.

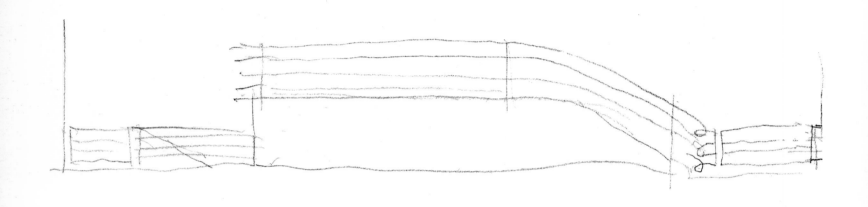

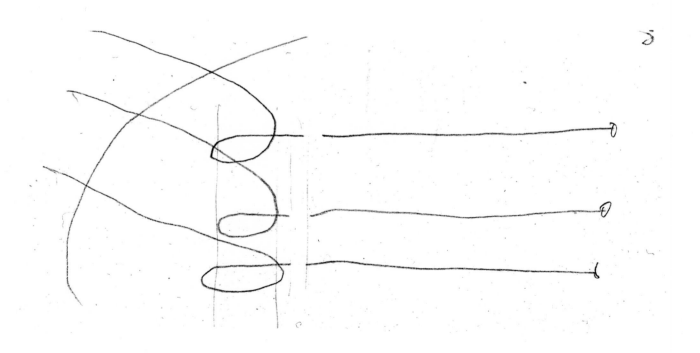

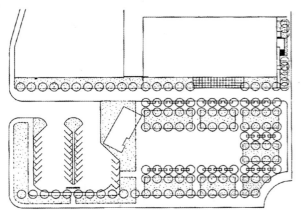

Site plan

Second floor

Roof plan

First floor

Fourth floor

Ground floor

Third floor

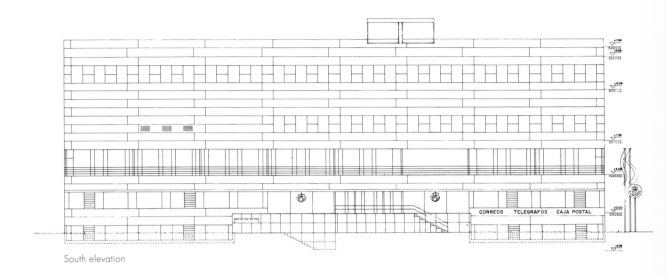

South elevation

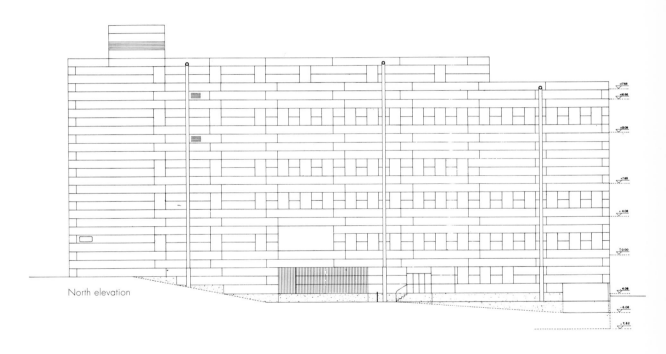

North elevation

East elevation

Site plan

Foundations

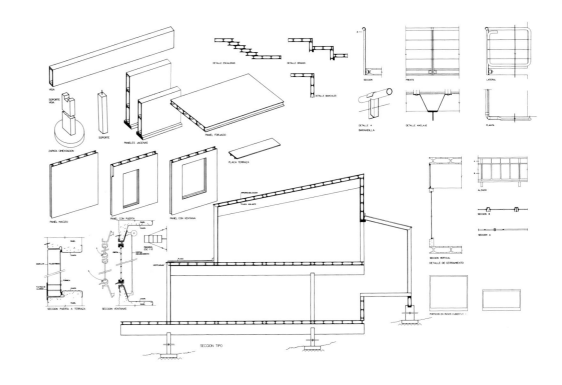

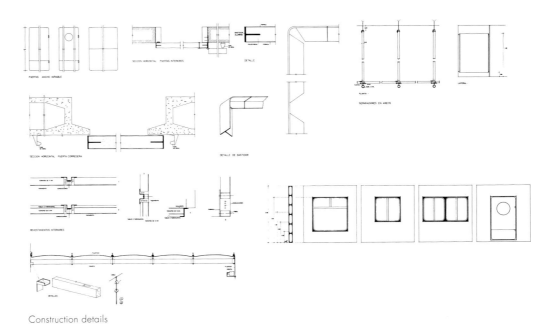

Construction details

Repetition of a volumetric module for multiple uses. Construction of pre-stressed concrete panels, with different interior finishes.

Windows, doors and details from the coachwork industry. Original general layout with vernacular influences from my home region: Galicia.

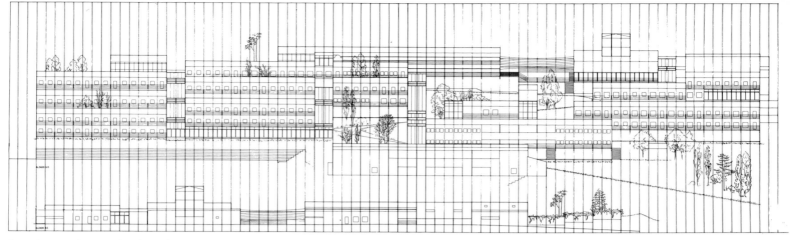

From above: northwest and southeast elevations

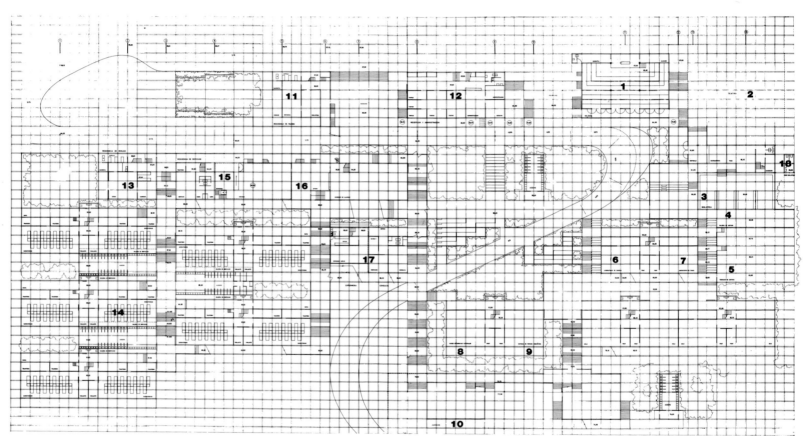

Ground floor

1. Church
2. Theatre
3. Library
4. Reading gallery
5. Reading terraces
6. Chemistry laboratories
7. Physics laboratories
8. Natural science museum
9. Fine arts museum
10. Games
11. Priests' residence
12. Reception and administration
13. Sisters' residence
14. Students' residence
15. Staff residence
16. Kitchen and dining room
17. Sick bay
18. Toilets

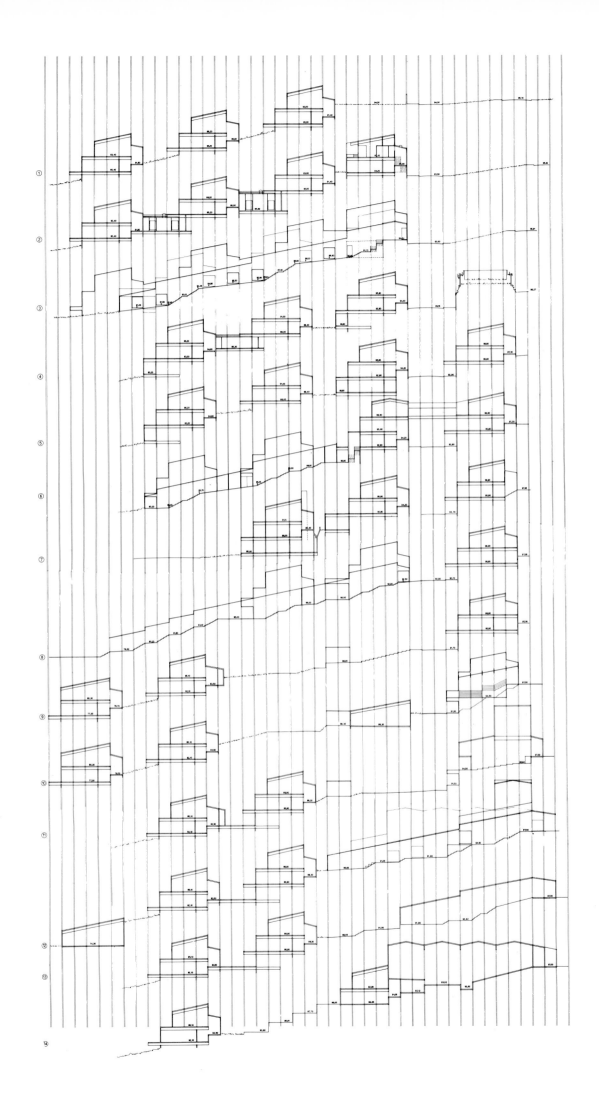

Site sections

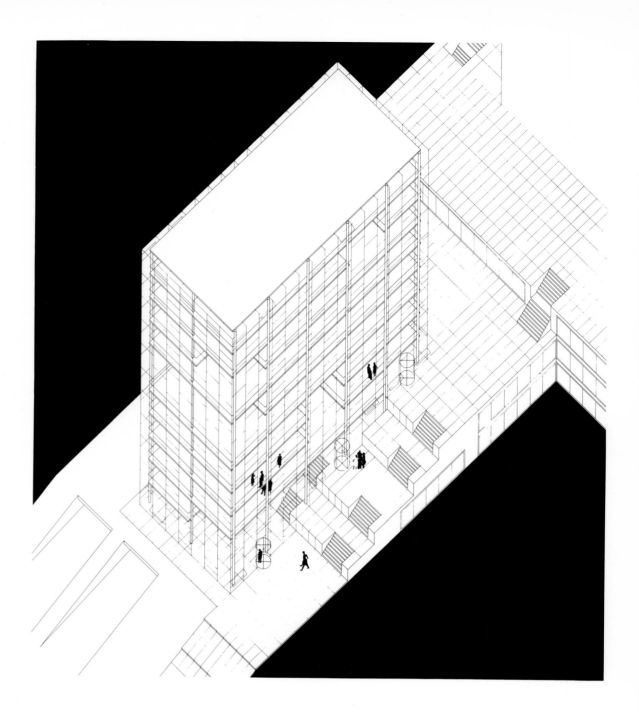

Competition project

There is a great beauty and freedom of interior to be found in a building under construction, especially if it is sited among large trees. This was the basic idea behind the project.

The building was designed to be open to the exterior. Its glass skin is separated from the floor slabs and fastened with brackets. Transoms and mullions are unnecessary, as the huge panes of glass are continuously sealed along a series of staggered joints.

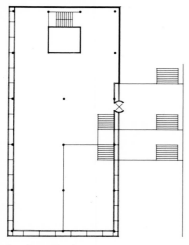

First floor of bank

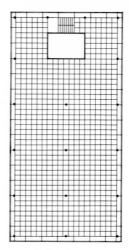

Typical office floor

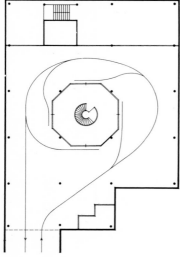

Public banking hall

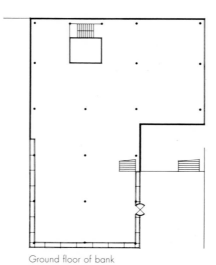

Ground floor of bank

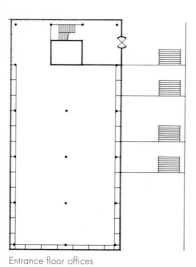

Entrance floor offices

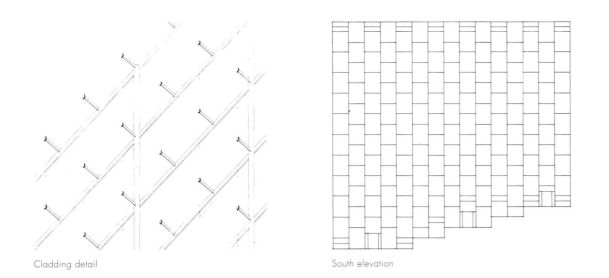

Cladding detail

South elevation

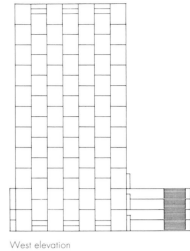

West elevation

Arvesu house Calle Doctor Arce, Madrid 1955

The house as a place of calm, of retreat from the world; a place to seek out the sun, the life-source; and, of course, the incontrovertible municipal regulations that established a five-metre setback on one side of the property and a three-metre setback on the other – these were the influences on the design.

If the architect had completely disregarded the client's wishes and followed his own instincts, there would be not a single window in what is commonly known as the facade.

The compromise: a heavy enclosure of solid brick with only a few small openings on to the street; and a light enclosure with large openings on to the more favourable orientation – the garden and the silence.

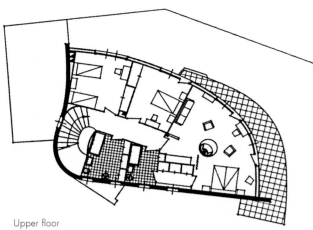

Upper floor

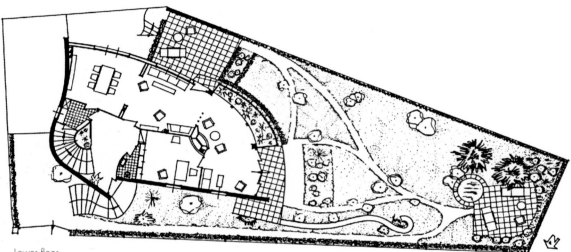

Lower floor

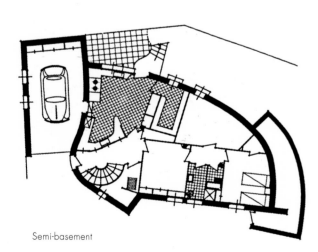

Semi-basement

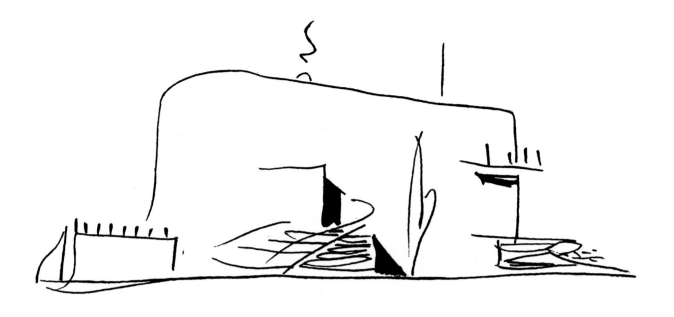

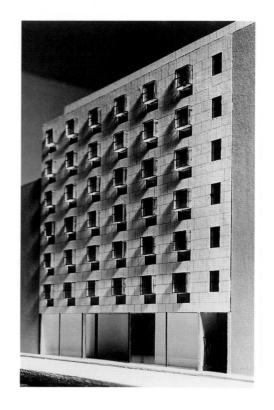

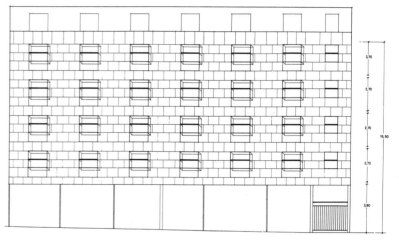

These are apartments with no great claims to novelty. In Salamanca, as in many Spanish cities, apartment-dwellers are interested in their fellow citizens. They find out about the life of the neighbourhood by keeping an eye on the street. They need to look out, consequently they need 'look-out places' – glazed bays, *miradores*.

Calle Prior is narrow, with no room for the usual kind of bays, so these were designed as small but effective and comfortable projections; they are tough, childproof even.

The facade is of Salamanca stone, treated in the traditional way: brush-hammered and flush-jointed. This type of stonework is being forgotten nowadays. More's the pity.

The stone facade rests on cantilevers. Below it, the entire ground floor along Calle Prior is enclosed with a continuous sheet of glass.

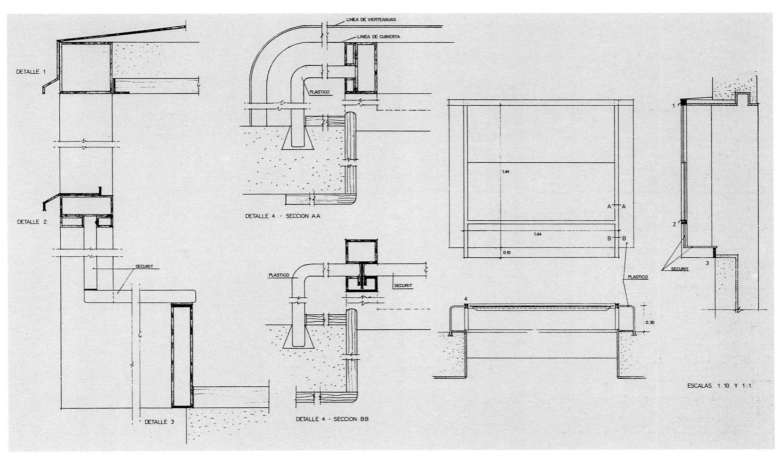

DETALLE 1

DETALLE 2

SECURIT

DETALLE 3

LINEA DE VIERTEAGUAS

LINEA DE CUBIERTA

PLASTICO

DETALLE 4 - SECCION A A

PLASTICO

SECURIT

DETALLE 4 - SECCION BB

1.44

1.44

0.10

A   A

B   B

PLASTICO

4

0.30

SECURIT

ESCALAS 1:10 Y 1:1

Details of bays

90

Guzmán house Algete, Madrid 1972

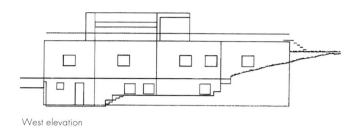

West elevation

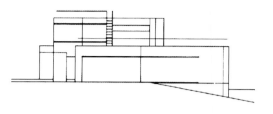

South elevation

The site is a trapezoid bounded by a road to the south and by the unique landscape of the Jarama river valley to the north. The house opens out to take advantage of the pleasant climate in spring, summer and autumn. Terraces link up its different levels. The whole effect is very much related to the landscape. Construction: mixed concrete and steel structure; brick walls dressed with brick tile.

One of the benefits of modern construction is that it allows us to make a truly open house which can also be truly closed. This may sound contradictory, but it is a genuine innovation. There is no fixed boundary between interior and exterior. The garden comes into the house.

Further considerations in the design were: orientation for light and views; the presence of the building form; privacy and security; an encompassing sense of comfort.

We sometimes talk about a building having a specific weight for a specific purpose. It is necessary to let the house hover, fly up, then come down to rest in its place. The house is a solid floating in magma.

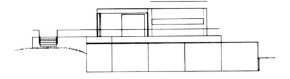

North elevation

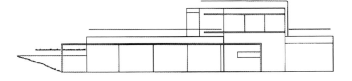

East elevation

Saarinen once said that Man's dwelling place could be represented by a sphere positioned half below ground, half above it. The part below the plane of the earth would be for rest, relaxation, gathering one's strength and thoughts; the part above it, for activity, acting on thoughts. The lower hemisphere would be of stone and earth; the upper one would be of transparent materials, glass.

As its inhabitants' thoughts became freer, the crystalline hemisphere would detach itself more and more from the earth until, breaking free, it would fly away – a whole new sphere, unstoppable. The sunken hemisphere would be similarly responsive, burrowing deeper into the earth as the need for rest became greater.

This was an image that I kept in my head for years until I found the precise conditions in which to give it physical form.

The starting point here is the horizontal plane, level 0. Below this the negative levels contain the rest areas, bedrooms and related spaces. Above the 0 plane there is at first nothing, then the living room and dining area – the places of activity. This brings us to a natural approach to construction and the use of materials. The lower part of the house, the refuge, is of heavy materials: concrete, brick and cladding. The upper part is of lightweight materials: steel, metal and glass panes, which give both the structure and its inhabitants the freedom to fly.

At the very top there is a terrace – a launching pad.

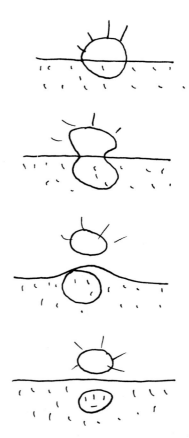

Graphic interpretation of a text by Saarinen

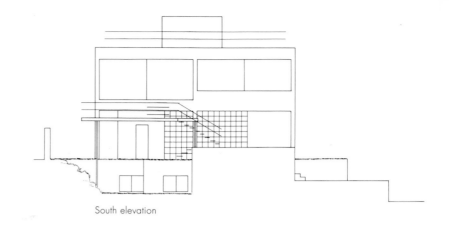

South elevation

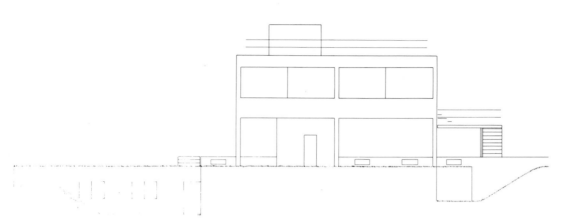

West elevation

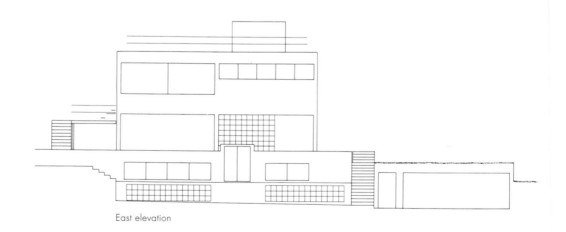

East elevation

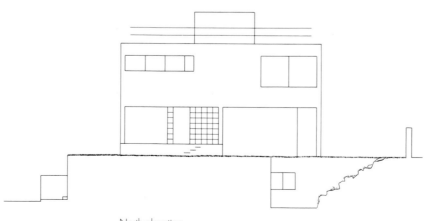

North elevation

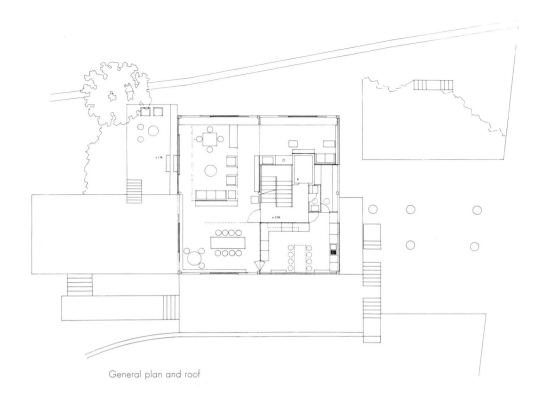

General plan and roof

Plan at levels -1.70 -2.55 and 3.50

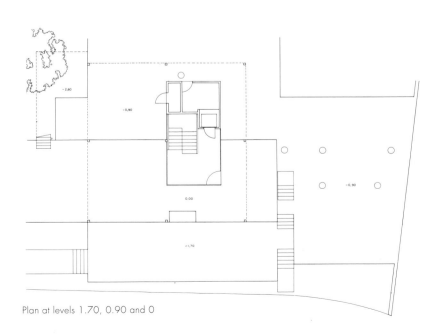

Plan at levels 1.70, 0.90 and 0

Design project
in collaboration with
Mauricio Sánchez-Bella

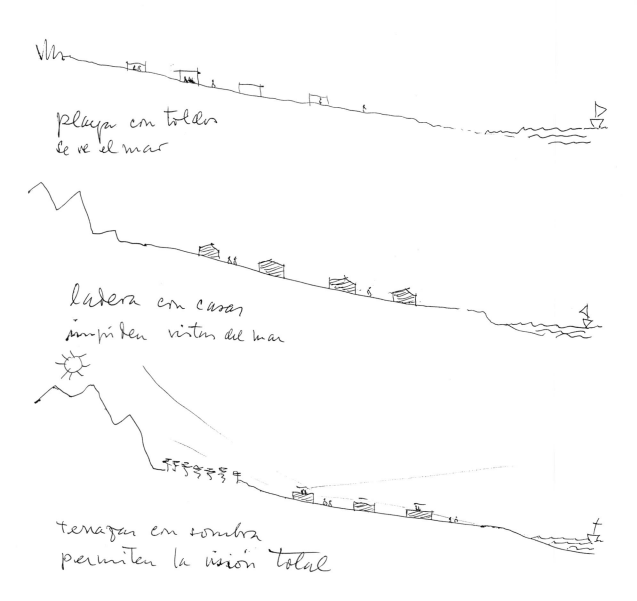

playa con toldos
se ve el mar

ladera con casas
impiden vistas del mar

terraza en sombra
permiten la visión total

Man is by nature territorial.

Traditionally, if the climate was propitious, he needed only to mark his territory superficially, in the manner of the lion's roar, the fox's scent. But if he wished to satisfy his innate desire for privacy, he had to have a sheltered place to work and rest. By making his home an enclosure Man attained all this, but lost Nature. So he looked for a way to recover it – if not wholly, at least in part.

Thus the courtyard was invented.

The courtyard can be found everywhere, from Pompeii through to Mies, and not least of all in Spain: it is set inside the house, if space permits; if not, it is adjacent, contiguous and defined by walls.

The intention here was to make an urban housing development with additional walls, which afford more privacy. The space inside is covered with vines, climbing plants and awnings. In this way the small plot of land acquires the character of a grand habitation.

The shaded terrace also acts as a kind of 'periscope', giving each house distant views of the mountains and the sea.

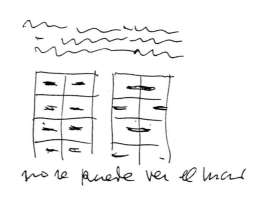

no se puede ver el mar

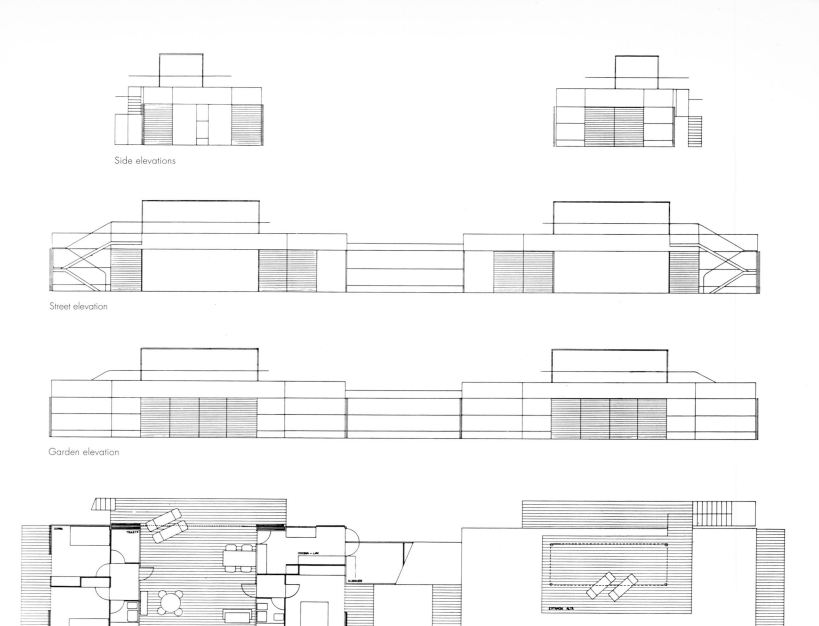

Side elevations

Street elevation

Garden elevation

Ground floor

Upper floor

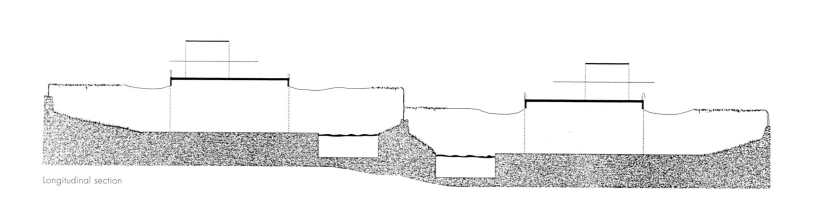

Longitudinal section

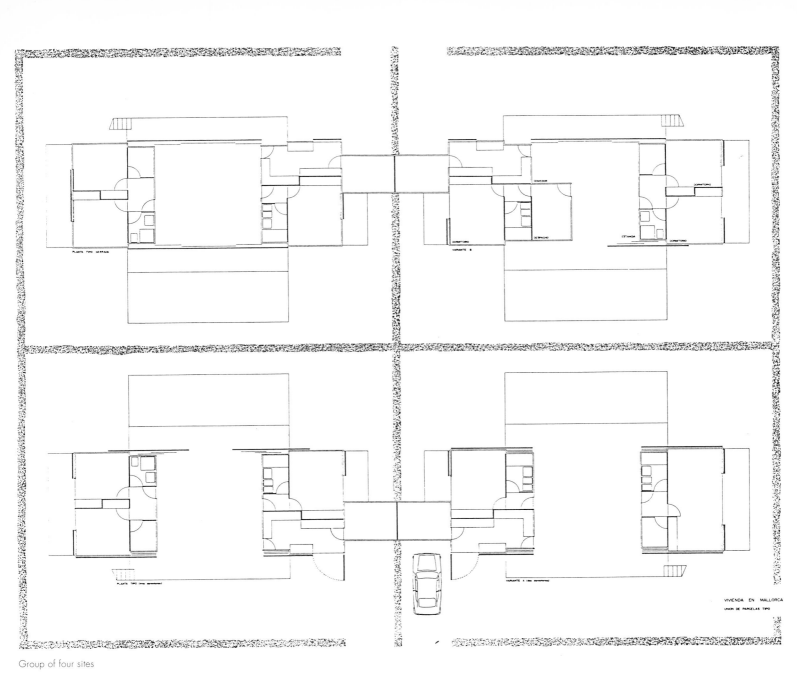

Group of four sites

Furniture

An architect solves problems. But he can impart a sense of beauty as well.

The size of living spaces has been enormously reduced, for both the well-to-do and those of limited means. One consequence of this has been the creation of multi-purpose furniture, also of a reduced scale: convertible tables, sofa-beds, fold-down tables, folding chairs, etc.

The table and two chairs shown here are intended to respond to these new requirements, these problems.

Two chairs

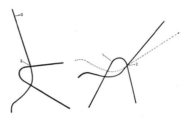 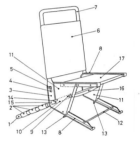

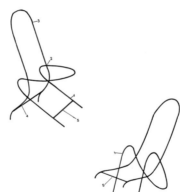 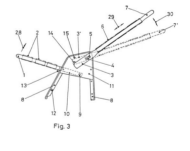

Fig. 3

Playing around with two of my wife's hairgrips I came up with a prototype for a chair. It turned out not to be very comfortable, and so was abandoned. However, I kept the basic idea of a chair that could be either upright or reclining, and started from scratch with the form, arriving after many changes, mainly simplifications, at recliner/chair B. This has the virtue of abstraction, as it arises

from an idea that was initially without form. It can be flat-packed and is easy to assemble and transport.

Having resolved chair B so conclusively, I went back to work on version A of the recliner and devised a hinge that made it practicable. It consists of two 'hairgrips' which rotate together around a common axis.

A table

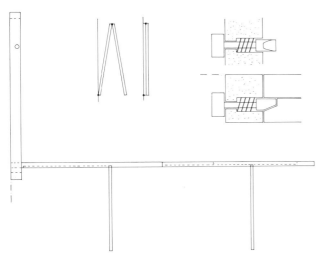

Most fitted tables come in a fixed, single size. By contrast this fold-down table can double in size, accommodating four/five people in its first position and eight/ten when fully extended. This is achieved by means of an ingenious system of supports of different lengths. The table can be fixed under the serving hatch between the kitchen and dining area, or folded back into a cupboard in the dining room, or used as a partition to divide up a room. In all cases, it offers an efficient solution for the combined living/dining room.

Furniture and fittings

Civil Government building,
Tarragona

Door handle

Maravillas Gymnasium,
Madrid

Window catch

Residential building,
Calle Prior, Salamanca

Buildings and projects of Alejandro de la Sota

1945

Single-family house
Ramón de Dios, Pontevedra   B

Single-family house Sr Pareja Deva,
Guipúzcoa, with Ricardo Abaurre   B

Agricultural training college
Gimenells, Lérida; agricultural engineers:
Angel Martínez Borque/José Baquero   B

Camisería Denis (shop) Madrid,
with Javier Lahuerta   B

1946

Eight homes Ronda, Málaga,
with Ricardo Abaurre   B

1947

Residential building Calle Alenza,
Madrid, with Ricardo Abaurre   B

1948

Municipal Savings Bank Vigo,
Pontevedra, with José María Iturriaga   C

Agricultural training college
Bastiagueiro, La Coruña   B

1950

Laboratories for Misión Biológica
Salcedo, Pontevedra   B

1951

SAM Dairies Salamanca;
agricultural engineer: Miguel Ramos   P

Single-family house Tangiers   P

1952

Two children's shops Madrid   B

Architect's own house
Avenida de los Toreros, 66, Madrid   B

1952–56

Aviaco administration & ticket offices
Palma de Mallorca, Santiago de
Compostela, La Coruña, Granada   B

1954

Local Government building La Coruña C

1955

Tax offices Tarragona   C

Esquivel village Seville   B

Fuencarral B. provisional housing
development Madrid   B

Arvesù house Madrid; demolished 1987

Agricultural engineers exhibition
Madrid   B

Andrade house Pontevedra   P

Building for the Provincial Savings
Bank Pontevedra   C

Poch house Sangenjo, Pontevedra   P

1956

Residential building Zamora   B

Villages of Entrerrios Valuengo
and La Bazana Badajoz   B

Pontevedra exposition pavilion
Madrid; temporary structure

Tax offices La Coruña, with Ramón
Vázquez Molezún and Antonio Tenreiro   C

1956–61

Civil Government building
Tarragona; restored by the architect
with José Llinás, 1987   C/B

1957

TABSA Aeronautical Plant Barajas,
Madrid; aeronautical engineer: Enrique de
Guzmán; engineer: Eusebio Rojas Marcos B

1957

Children's summer home
Miraflores de la Sierra, Madrid,
with José Antonio Corrales and Ramón
Vázquez Molezún; altered without the
architect's supervision

1958

Parish centre Vitoria   P

Parish centre San Estéban Protomártir   C

Restoration of single-family house
Imporex, S.A., Seville   P

Parish centre Combarro, Pontevedra   P

1959

Residential building Calle Narváez,
Madrid   P

Santa María School Madrid   C

Velázquez house Pozuelo, Madrid   B

1961

Swimming pools El Escorial, Madrid   B

Spanish Pavilion New York World's Fair,
with Francisco Fernández Longoria and
Bernardo Yncenga   C

CLESA Dairy Madrid;
agricultural engineer: Manuel Ramos   B

Maravillas Gymnasium Madrid;
engineer: Eusebio Rojas Marcos   B

1963

Institute of Non-ferrous Materials
Madrid   P

Residential building Salamanca;
altered without architect's supervision, 1988

Metal research and testing bays for
CENIM University campus, Madrid   B

Architect's house Avenida de América,
Madrid   B

1964

Church Nantes, Pontevedra   P

Aparicio house (snail house)
Canillejas, Madrid   P

Emigrants' housing Irún, Guipúzcoa   B

Varela house Collado Mediano,
Villalba, Madrid   B

Pazó house Sangenjo, Pontevedra   P

Sports facilities for the National
Sports Delegation   C

1965

Residential development
Bahía Bella, Mar Menor, Murcia   P

Las Palmeras residential
development Málaga   P

1966

Sports pavilion Pontevedra; altered
without the architect's supervision, 1987

1967

César Carlos hall of residence
University campus, Madrid;
restored with J. Balenciaga, 1988   P

Residential college for the
Provincial Savings Bank Orense   P

House and clinic for Dr Corbal
Orense   P

Housing Santander   P

Olmedo house La Caeyra, Pontevedra   P

1968

Housing block Calle O'Donell Madrid   P

1970

Bankunión headquarters Madrid   C

1971

Law school Granada   P

1972

Hall of residence Salamanca   P

Guzmán house Algete, Madrid   B

Residential building
Calle Gondomar, Pontevedra   B

School building Seville   C

1974

Marianist school La Coruña   B

1975

Calculation unit for the Postal Savings
Bank Madrid, with Juan Capella   B

Aviaco headquarters Madrid   C

1976

Dominguez house Pontevedra   B

1977

Residential building San Blas, Madrid P

Post Office and Savings Bank
building Almendralejo, Badajoz   P

Housing development
Calle Velázquez, Madrid   P

1984

Post Office and Telecommunications
building León   B

Provincial Museum León   P

Housing development Alcudia, Mallorca,
with Mauricio Sánchez-Bella   P

Parish centre Badajoz,
with Gerardo Ayala   P

1985

Congress and concert hall Salamanca C

1986

Sports village Salamanca,
with A. Freire, J. Marcos, E. Sánchez Gil,
I. Vicente, J. Vicente   C

Residential building on the M-30
Madrid   C

Inserso headquarters Madrid   C

MOPU gallery Madrid   B

Residential and office building
Gran Via de San Francisco, Madrid   B

1987

Extension of the Parliament building
Madrid   C

Court building Zaragoza   B

New Chancellery and Spanish
Embassy to the OECD Paris   P

1988

Houses Lorca, Murcia   P

1990

Provincial Museum León; second project

1991

Restoration and extension of the
Cabildo Insular Las Palmas,
Canary Islands   B

1993

University library
Santiago de Compostela   B

Key: B built, P project, C competition